M

LUCIEN GOLDMANN

Essays on Method in the Sociology of Literature

Translated and edited by
William Q. Boelhower

TELOS PRESS
ST. LOUIS, MO.

ISBN: 0-914386-19-0 cloth
       0-914386-20-4 paper

Library of Congress Card Number: 79-89567

Manufactured in the United States of America

Table of Contents

Introduction, by William Q. Boelhower   5

Essays on Method in the Sociology of Literature

1. Subject and Object in the Human Sciences   35

2. The Epistemology of Sociology   55

3. The Concept of Significant Structure
   in the History of Culture   75

4. The Social Structure and the Collective
   Consciousness of Structure   85

5. The Subject of the Cultural Creation   91

6. Theses on the Use of the Concept "World View"
   in the History of Philosophy   111

7. Sociological and Cultural Denunciation   117

8. Genetic Structuralism and Stylistic Analysis   141

Index   157

Introduction

The list of English translations and articles dealing with Lucien Goldmann's attempts to elaborate a sociological aesthetics clearly shows an increasing familiarity with his genetic structuralism and the corresponding need to come to an accurate definition of his theoretical contribution, especially in the field of literary method.[1] Unfortunately, too many scholars have ignored the fact that Goldmann was above all an essayist. Specific works by Goldmann almost always have a tentative, polemical or even schematic character. Consequently, while his thought no longer needs to be introduced to the English-reading public, it is evident from the very nature of these introductions (which are usually limited to a consideration of *The Hidden God* and *Toward a Sociology of the Novel*) that his work needs to be seen in its entirety to be correctly evaluated.[2] There is a great deal of confusion and inaccurate criticism concerning the nature of certain categories that make up what Goldmann believed to be a formal method, precisely because only parts of his work are taken into account.[3] Goldmann himself is partly to blame for this,

---

1. A bibliography of Goldmann's work available in English (including essays about him) appears in Goldmann's *Cultural Creation in Modern Society* (Telos Press: St. Louis, 1976). Since then, Routledge & Kegan Paul has published my translation of Goldmann's *Lukacs and Heidegger* (1977). Goldmann's crucial essay, "The Epistemology of Sociology," also has appeared since then, in *Telos* 30 (Winter 1976-77). For the full list of Goldmann's scattered essays, see Eduard Tell's definitive bibliography, originally published in *Revue de l'institut de sociologie*, 3-4 (Brussels, 1973), pp. 787-806.

2. The best introductions to Goldmann's work are Raymond Williams' essay in *New Left Review*, 67 (June 1971), pp. 3-18; Jacques Leenhardt's essay in *Revue d'Esthétique*, 2 (1971), pp. 113-128; Jean-Michel Palmier's essay in *Esthétique et Marxisme* (Union Générale d'Edition: Paris, 1974), pp. 107-188.

3. See M. Crouzet's essay, "Racine et le marxisme en histoire littéraire," *La nouvelle critique* (November 1956), pp. 61-83. Here he accuses Goldmann of being eclectic, of mixing Marxism with certain neo-Kantian ideas implying a formal imposition of categories on his texts in an *a priori* fashion smacking of idealism.

insofar as he never clearly ordered or qualified his various borrowings — mainly from Lukacs, Marx and Piaget — in other words, he never carried out his intention to order his aesthetics in a systematic fashion as, for example, Lukacs and Adorno did.[4]

On the other hand, there has been too much haste in categorizing Goldmann. He is generally considered simply a disciple of the early Lukacs, as a fellow victim of the idealism in Lukacs' Marxism that resulted from Lukacs' inability to overcome his early neo-Kantian heritage. (Lukacs once belonged to the Heidelberg circle of Simmel, Rickert, Lask and Weber.)[5] Attempts to fix Goldmann's method in its Lukacsian dimensions (and here one can cite Grahl's introduction to *Cultural Creation in Modern Society* as the latest example) fail because they neglect crucial texts, most of which have been inaccessible or have been ignored to accommodate the speculative ambience of Lukacs the philosopher.

The essays presented here, then, are chosen for their contribution to a picture of a more positive and sociologically oriented Goldmann — a thinker who achieved intellectual autonomy by giving a new dimension to his "Lukacsian" categories. This he has done by giving them a coherent anthropological basis in Piaget's interactionist epistemology. Indeed, it is through Piaget's influence that he has made Lukacs less idealistic for methodological purposes. This is Goldmann's unique contribution toward an interdisciplinary sociology of cultural creations. As Goldmann said in an interview, "I am less a speculative philosopher — I am not one at all — than I am a sociologist, a man of science who tries both to do concrete research and to isolate a positive method for the study of human and social facts."[6]

Besides bearing out this empirical dimension (one should point out that Lukacs was never concerned with elaborating a model of literary criticism as Goldmann and contemporary French critics

---

4. According to Leenhardt, in the essay mentioned above, Goldmann was thinking about ordering his model into a theoretical system.

5. See De Feo's *Weber e Lukacs* (De Donato: Bari, 1970); Laura Boella's *Il Giovane Lukacs* (De Donato: Bari, 1977) and the special issue of *Aut Aut* (January-April 1977) on Lukacs as seen by the members of the Budapest School.

6. "Structuralisme, marxisme, existentialisme," *L'Homme et la Société*, 2 (1966), p. 109.

were), these same "Piagetian" essays are also crucial for documenting an even more important fact: namely, that Goldmann succeeded implicitly in providing for his categories to be made into a systematic dialectical model. In other words, they can be brought together formally in a theoretically coherent fashion. In fact, his primary contribution lies here. As Goldmann says, "We have also defined the positive human sciences and more exactly the Marxist method by means of a nearly identical term (which, moreover, we have borrowed from Jean Piaget), that of *genetic structuralism.*"[7] According to Goldmann, it is Piaget, "not at all...influenced by Marx, who has empirically discovered in his research laboratory nearly all of the fundamental positions Marx had formulated a hundred years earlier in the domain of the social sciences."[8]

Given this new emphasis on Goldmann's Piagetian context and the possibility of formally organizing his categories on this basis, then, it remains to point out Goldmann's use of certain categories borrowed from Lukacs and to order them into the model he intended. It is hoped that this approach will enable the reader to place the particular heuristic categories of single essays into a theoretical framework where they are related to other such categories. (Thus, while the essay "Subject and Object in the Human Sciences" introduces the reader to the delicate theoretical balance Goldmann achieved, the categories presented there are given a more rigorous order in the following essay, "The Epistemology of Sociology.")[9]

The major advantage, but also the major difficulty, of the sociology of literature in general lies in its recognizing the need to

---

7. *Marxisme et sciences humaines* (Gallimard: Paris, 1970), p. 246.

8. *Entretiens sur les notions de génèse et de structure* (Mouton: The Hague, 1965), p. 15. The two major Goldmann essays that most explicitly express his debt to Piaget are "The Epistemology of Sociology" (in this volume) and "Jean Piaget et la philosophie," *Cahiers Vilfredo Pareto*, 10 (1966), pp. 5-23. There are also two essays on Piaget in Goldmann's *Recherches Dialectiques* (Gallimard: Paris, 1959).

9. The next step would be to use the model in concrete research and then, in terms of current theoretical developments, to incorporate it into the complementary research of Jan Mukarovsky and Jurij Lotman and Boris Uspenskij of the School of Tartu, all of whom attempt to elaborate a semiology of cultural creations using methods strikingly similar to Goldmann's genetic structuralism. See Jan Mukarovsky, *Il Significato dell'Estetica* (Einaudi: Turin, 1973); Jurij Lotman, *La Struttura del Testo Poetico* (Mursia: Milan, 1972); Lotman and Boris Uspenskij, *Semiotica e Cultura* (Riccardo Ricciardi: Milan, 1975); Lotman and Uspenskij, *Tipologia della Cultura* (Bompiani: Milan, 1975).

develop synoptic categories that can link two heterogeneous levels — society and literature or history and aesthetics. This need is expressed by Lotman: "Just as semiotic relations require not only a text but also a language, so the artistic work, considered alone, without any cultural context, without a definite system of cultural codes, is like an 'inscription on a tomb in an unknown language'."[10] Given this need, what tools allow the theoretical grounding of the correspondences between such levels? While dialectical materialism has always been the most sophisticated method of linking art and society, it is precisely Goldmann's contribution to have taken this much embattled heritage and to have formed paradigmatic categories that allow one to pass back and forth between these two levels, but in a non-mechanistic fashion. Only with such dialectical categories could he have avoided privileging either the discipline of sociology or that of aesthetics.

In order to conceptualize the levels of the cultural creation of society, the *sine qua non* of a valid sociological aesthetics, Goldmann collected certain macro-analytical categories (totality, world view, form, the transindividual subject and possible consciousness-objective possibility) from Lukacs and grounded them in a series of positive and anthropological categories taken from Piaget (significant structure, function, the structuration-destructuration process, the epistemological circle of the subject and object, equilibrium). His intention was to convert the categories that Lukacs used in a philosophical and merely descriptive way into methodological prototypes that would prove to be highly functional, rather than ideological instruments. And here we are faced with a major difference between the two thinkers: Lukacs was pre-eminently a philosopher, Goldmann a sociologist.

This distinction becomes more apparent when Goldmann's use of Piaget's genetic epistemology to formalize his Lukacsian categories is put in its proper perspective. In "Introduction aux premiers écrits de Georges Lukacs,"[11] Goldmann explains that the term "significant structure" is Lukacs' most important contribution to the attempt to make the human sciences positive.

---

10. Lotman, *La Struttura del Testo Poetico*, p. 335.
11. In *Les Temps Modernes* (August 1962).

Later, in the same article, however, he admits that Lukacs never used this term but, instead, used the concept "form" in *The Soul and the Forms* and a similar concept, "totality," in *History and Class Consciousness* — and, one might add, "ideal type" in *Theory of the Novel*. He points out that "form" stands for a Husserlian essence in Lukacs' existential work, while Lukacs himself admits the Kantianism of the typological method in *Theory of the Novel*.[12] In fact, as Goldmann observes in "The Concept of the Significant Structure in the History of Culture," the term significant structure, which is the basic category of Goldmann's model, derives from Piaget's *Etudes d'epistemologie genetique*, vol. II, *Logique et equilibre*. In *The Hidden God*, where Goldmann's major purpose is "to develop a scientific method for the study of literary and philosophical works," he writes, "The central idea of this book is that facts concerning man always form themselves into significant global structures, which are at one and the same time practical, theoretical and emotive, and that these structures can be studied in a scientific manner, that is to say, they can be both explained and understood only within a practical perspective based on the acceptance of a certain set of values."[13] The aspect that the concept of significant structure provides Goldmann's model is a functionality and positiveness not found in the Lukacs who inspired Goldmann. The methodological intent of *The Hidden God* is to present structures (at the artistic and extra-artistic levels) entirely in a historical perspective. "I set out from the fundamental principle of dialectical materialism, that the knowledge of empirical facts remains abstract and superficial as long as it is not made concrete by its integration into a whole and that only this act of integration can enable us to go beyond the incomplete and abstract phenomenon in order to arrive at its concrete essence, and thus, implicitly, at its meaning."[14] This circular process involving the act of insertion is grounded anthropologically by Goldmann's use

---

12. Cf. Boella, *Il giovane Lukacs, op.cit.*, pp. 22ff., where she shows the two separate levels of investigation Lukacs carries out — one socio-historical, the other metaphysical-existential — because he always projects two separate realities: historical becoming and a metaphysical and normative universality. The socio-historical level of investigation is purely descriptive and auxiliary and is in conflict with the forms and their investigation.
13. *The Hidden God* (Routledge & Kegan Paul: London, 1967), p. ix.
14. *Ibid.*, p. 7.

of Piaget's concepts of assimilation and accommodation[15] and by his notion of facts in the human sciences as constructions that are made by transindividual subjects into relative totalities across structuring and destructuring processes.[16] In other words, facts are never immediate givens. They can be interpreted in a positive way only if one refers them to their significant englobing structures and to the activity of human groups responsible for the genesis of these structures. As György Markus says, Lukacs lacked this methodological coherence insofar as he maintained a constant parallelism (involving two different types of analysis) between a metaphysical-existential level, that of form, and the historical level.[17] In Lukacs' use of form there is an atemporal aspect that necessarily creates a dualism between it and a socio-historical analysis of a given epoch.

Perhaps at this point, one should mention that Goldmann has a constructivist view of structures (whether they pertain to history or to cultural creations) rather than a preconstructed view of them, as Lukacs has — if the term "form" is substituted for structure. For Goldmann, structures do not have idealistic or neo-Kantian elements. It is men acting collectively along class lines who create structures and transform them.[18] Nor need one appeal to a metaphysical level to analyze structures. In doing so, one naturally opens oneself to an epistemological dualism, where structures are partly dehistoricized and, thus, are made partly dysfunctional.

Goldmann writes, "Now, one of the most important discussions in the human sciences today is that of knowing whether men or structures generate historical transformations...; genetic structuralism asserts that structures, being a universal aspect of all human thought, sensibility or behavior, could in no instance replace man as a historical subject."[19] (This perspective also distinguishes Goldmann from many structuralists and relates him

---

15. *Ibid.*, p. 15.
16. See "The Subject of the Cultural Creation" in this volume and "The Topicality of the Question of the Subject" in *Lukacs and Heidegger, op.cit.*, pp. 86-98.
17. *Aut Aut* (January-April 1977), p. 153.
18. See Goldmann's "The Social Structure and the Collective Consciousness of Structures" in this volume.
19. *Linguaggi nella Società e nella Technica* (Edizioni di Communità: Milan, 1970), p. 152. Goldmann's essay there is entitled "Structuralisme génétique et analyse stylistique," pp. 143-161.

to certain contemporary semiologists.) The literary work, seen as a structure, must be related to historical subjects, not to some sphere outside history. It is in this way that a text's sociality and communicability can be captured, and it is here that one finds Goldmann's positioning of the relationship between art and society. To deny this position would be to abandon the literary text in its socio-aesthetic unity to an idealist position that ignores the text as praxis. The latter position would drape the text in an irrational and mystifying veil, thereby casting cultural creations into a subjective vacuum characterized by the meta-historical and the extra-cultural. Objectivity would, in this case, be reduced to the faculty of intuition. To avoid such mystifications, Goldmann goes back to certain anthropological principles. He writes: "It seems to me that these three basic characteristics of human behavior, that is: (1) man's tendency to adapt himself to his milieu and, thus, the significant and rational character of his behavior in relation to it, (2) man's tendency to coherence and to global structuring processes, (3) the dynamic character of his behavior and the modifying tendency of the structure of which he is a part, as well as the developmental tendency of the latter, are found at the base of all positive research into the literary creation."[20]

On the basis of this constructivist view of structures, then, Goldmann provides a new positive perspective for the remaining Lukacsian, or idealist, categories having a neo-Kantian quality: totality, world view, and possible consciousness-objective possibility. Even the Marxist orientation of Lukacs' *History and Class Consciousness*, the major category of the book being that of totality, is idealist and in a continuum with his early work. Goldmann, of course, is clearly aware of the fact and says so in his work *Lukacs and Heidegger* and in his "Introduction aux premiers écrits de Georges Lukacs." As he indicates in the latter, the merit of Lukacs' work from 1923 on is to have made basic methodological principles available to later researchers. Goldmann realizes that Lukacs' notion of totality in *History and Class Consciousness* is dogmatic. It functions in an *a priori* fashion, presuming that the self-awareness of the working class

---

20. *Littérature et société* (Editions de l'institut de sociologie: Brussels, 1967), p. 203.

would be sufficient to bring about a total and transparent identity between subject and object. In this sense, it is a pre-constructive category, functioning almost as if it were an essence beyond historical vicissitudes. This is *not* the case with Goldmann for the obvious reason that totality, always a relative structure, is bound to the praxis and conflict of transindividual subjects wholly within a given society. Goldmann uses totality for its methodological potential only, thus making it less idealistic. He speaks of the partial identity of the subject and object and of the need to recognize mediations between them. Totality is never a static or completely objectivized concept, since it is always in the process of being structured or destructured. Goldmann uses Piaget's term "equilibrium" to describe the dynamic and open nature of a relative totality at a given moment.

As for world view, Lukacs is much closer to Dilthey's use of this concept, used to describe the unitary spirit of an epoch, than is Goldmann. Boella notes that the early Lukacs uses this concept in a quasi-nominalistic way peculiar to Max Weber and as a formal organizational principle of reality, a *medium* through which the closed world of the literary text is built.[21] Certainly, Lukacs uses this concept in an abstract and merely descriptive way in comparison to Goldmann, who wishes to make of it a rigorously accountable category by relating it to precise social groups. In this respect, given the conditioning presence of *Lebensphilosophie* in Lukacs' early thought, Lukacs did not go beyond using this category in a philosophical and existential way. Generally speaking, a *Weltanschauung* is what unifies life in all of its dimensions and, in the aesthetic sphere, it is the principle of style in given artistic forms. Without saying how, Lukacs gives the concept of world view a totalizing power. Thus, it becomes the scheme in which life and the forms are related symbolically. Of course, one is still left with the same methodological dualism mentioned earlier in the discussion of Lukacs' forms. As Boella says, the level of causality between the spirit of an epoch and an aesthetic form is not methodological, but historical and philo-sophical. The opposite is true with respect to Goldmann's use of the concept, as the essay "Theses on the Use of the Concept 'World View'..." demonstrates.

21. Boella, *Il Giovane Lukacs, op.cit.*, pp. 24-26, 30, 63.

The final Lukacsian categories that Goldmann used for his model (possible consciousness-objective possibility and the transindividual subject) derive from *History and Class Consciousness*. Although the terms possible consciousness and objective possibility have their origins in Max Weber's sociology of ideal types, Lukacs and Goldmann make their conceptual status depend on the notion of the transindividual subject (social class, groups). It is through the theory and praxis of these subjects that one finds a series of dialectical mediations between the concrete and the abstract level that avoid dissolving the former into logical categories in a unilateral way. In fact, Weber's method remains formal and analytical where Goldmann's is dialectical. The possible consciousness of a transindividual subject, the theoretical determination of the possibilities of changing reality at the structural level (I am referring to Marx's use of structure), is based on the principle that new relations cannot be imposed before the material conditions for them are formed. According to Goldmann, whether speaking of new or old relations, one can organize them and make them coherent only with respect to transindividual subjects.[22] As he says, however, "Even today (1968), Lukacs conceives of work and action as starting from global history but, contrary to former practice, he no longer connects its origin to the praxis of groups. . . ."[23] In his concrete analysis of literature, Lukacs never used these concepts for heuristic purposes, which is exactly what Goldmann set out to do. Indeed, Goldmann considered the concept of possible consciousness an essential part of his aesthetic model. He used it to stress not only the critical role and the relative autonomy of art in relation to society, but to clarify the conflictual, utopian and fantastic elements of a cultural creation. Like Antonio Gramsci, whose work he knew, Goldmann recognized the dynamic role of the intellectual, the artist, in relation to society. According to genetic structuralism, the literary work is a constitutive element of social consciousness and is less related to the level of the real consciousness of transindividual subjects than it is to their possible consciousness. At this mediating level, one is far from a mechanistic or simply mimetic theory of the art-society relation.

---

22. *Lukacs and Heidegger, op.cit.*, pp. 81, 82.
23. *Ibid.*, p. 90.

By ignoring Goldmann's total model, however, many critics have accused him of a vulgar sociologism, especially in reference to his use of the notion of homology in *Toward a Sociology of the Novel.*

Even there, however, one finds no emanationist theory of causality used to explain the formal origins of a literary work. As Goldmann says in *Recherches dialectiques*, "The dependence of major philosophical systems and works of art on the economic base is certainly a reality, but, on the one hand, it is far from being unilateral (Marx and Engels have often underlined the inverse influence of ideological and spiritual factors on the economic sphere), and on the other hand, it is extremely complex, indirect and masked, and above all, it does not take anything from the proper reality of the philosophical or artistic work under study."[24] The concepts of possible consciousness and objective possibility, as they are linked to the concept of the transindividual subject, demonstrate Goldmann's rigorous efforts to emphasize the complexity of the mediations between two different structural levels.

It now remains for the reader to see the exact synthesis Goldmann brought about by bringing these variously derived concepts into a genetic structuralist model, his lasting contribution to the sociology of literature.

Significant structure

In "The Concept of the Significant Structure in the History of Culture," Goldmann calls significant structure his principal research tool for understanding the human sciences. As a concept, though, it is based on the virtual and actual tendencies of human reality both on the superstructural and structural levels, Marx's theory and praxis tandem. In this sense, the category has a normative function based on specific anthropological observations that Goldmann synthesizes from Piaget's genetic psychology and Marx's dialectical theory. He characterizes cultural creations and transindividual subjects as significant structures and analyzes them on the level of their

---

24. Goldmann writes: "In fact, a certain distance is necessary between the individual who expresses a world vision and the group which implicitly elaborates the possibility of this vision in its praxis." *Ibid.*, p. 85.

mental categories and on the level of historical praxis. Crucial for the sociology of literature, these two levels (superstructural and structural) are dialectically related. The significant structure of a literary work and that of the mental categories making up the collective consciousness of transindividual subjects are intelligibly and necessarily related on the basis of their mutual definition as significant structures. In other words, the concept homogenizes Goldmann's genetic structuralism by pointing to the homologous relationship bletween structures of qualitatively different levels.

By joining Piaget's psychological conclusions on the "adaptive nature of intelligence" with dialectical materialism, Goldmann succeeds in grasping the psychological and sociological reality of human behavior.[25] For him, human behavior can be characterized as a coherent (structured) response to problems posed by man's relation to his fellow men and to his environment. This dialectical relationship, in which the mental categories of consciousness are strictly and reciprocally linked to praxis, describes what he calls pansignification.[26] Any given human act (imaginative, theoretical, practical, emotional) proves to be significant when inserted into a broader totality wherein its functional necessity is illuminated. To explain this meaningfulness on the social level of human reality, Goldmann relies on Piaget's description of the cycle of assimilation and accommodation. The first describes "the action of the organism on the objects surrounding it, insofar as this depends on previous behavior bearing upon the same objects or similar ones."[27] In *Lo Strutturalismo*, Piaget says, "The essential function (in the biological sense of the word) which leads to the formation of structures is that of 'assimilation,'...the generator of schemes, in fact, and thus of structures."[28] Accommodation accounts for the action of the environment upon the individual or group. In this instance, the assimilating process is modified to permit the individual to adjust to his environment. The entire cycle accounts for the significance of the concept of structure and is nothing

25. Cf. Goldmann, "Jean Piaget and Philosophy," p. 158.
26. Cf. "The Subject of Cultural Creation," and Goldmann's "Structure: réalité humaine et concept méthodologique," in R. Macksey and E. Donato, eds., *The Languages of Criticism and the Sciences of Man* (Johns Hopkins University Press: Baltimore, 1970), pp. 323ff.
27. Goldmann, "Jean Piaget and Philosophy," p. 158.
28. Piaget, *Lo Strutturalismo* (Il Saggiatore: Milan, 1968), p. 102.

other than the anthropological description of the subject-object circle; that is, the indissoluble link between a subject seeking a coherent balance with his environment, and a social context forever requiring the subject to restructure this balance. Marx, in reference to social classes, called this cycle that results in significant structures theoretical praxis.

Goldmann, however, prefers to use Piaget's terminology for his own model.[29] Following Piaget, he writes, "Structure is essentially defined by the necessity to fulfill a function in a certain situation," and again, "structures are born from events and from the everyday behavior of individuals.... Except for the most formal characteristics, there is no permanence in these structures."[30] Like Piaget, Goldmann prefers to speak of structuring processes rather than structures. As he explains in "The Epistemology of Sociology," there is only the ongoing process of structuration (assimilation) and destructuration (accommodation) which, at best, ends in a relative equilibrium and coherence. Through this preference he indicates his rejection of a merely static, synchronic notion of structure. *"Structure, significance* and *function* thus appear as three inseparable and complementary scientific concepts,"* Goldmann writes, for the simple reason that *"structure* exists by means of its significant character, which results from its aptitude to fulfill a *function."* He continues, *"Functions* could only be fulfilled by *structures*, and structures are *significant* to the extent that they are apt to fulfill a function."[31]

Granted that biological, psychological and sociological reality, as explored by Piaget and Marx, can be described by the category significant structure, Goldmann goes on to explain its *theoretical* use for the sociology of literature. As already indicated, this second aspect of the category is based on the epistemological circle of the subject and object or, to put it another way, on the dialectical unity of theory and praxis. At this point, Goldmann ingeniously employs the results of Piaget's laboratory research to verify the same operative principles in Marxism, only on a sociological level. Basically, this involves other categories of his

---

29. "Jean Piaget and Philosophy," p. 178.

30. *The Languages of Criticism*, pp. 100, 99.

31. These three quotations are from "Structure: réalité humaine et concept méthodologique," *The Languages of Criticism*, p. 324.

model, especially those of the transindividual subject and totality. According to Goldmann, man is a subject who is structured by an aggregate of mental categories that he has not created, but which come to him as part of a determinate world view. In order to understand the constructed subject at this often non-conscious level of meaning (Karl Mannheim calls this the documentary level), Goldmann inserts him into an encompassing structure of a transindividual subject. As a result, the pattern of mental categories becomes intelligible. Marx spoke of the need to explain the construction of groups that make history. These, too, are structured by their attempts to give coherent responses to the aggregate of problems posed by their relations to their environment (see "The Epistemology of Sociology"). The praxis of a social class as well as its theory represent attempts to arrive at an equilibrium through its interaction with other collective subjects and with the natural environment. The transindividual subject, then, is an encompassing structure of the individual and provides a way for understanding the structure of the individual's mental categories. The alternative of certain structuralist methods, for example, is that of arbitrarily and irrationally reducing the intelligibility of these categories to an internal analytical description, implying that the understanding of a structure is identical to its interpretation.

A social class, in turn, can be encompassed by the totality of social classes making up a society. The operative principle here is that one can best understand a significant structure by inserting it dialectically into its most immediately encompassing structure. Furthermore, it is transindividual subjects, above all, who elaborate world views, a process impossible for the individual to achieve. Goldmann speaks of social classes when describing praxis directed at a global structuring of society. In "Jean Piaget et philosophie," an essay in *Cahiers Vilfredo Pareto*, he also explains that in linking world views to social classes, he escapes both the meta-historical instrumentalization of Dilthey and the existential instrumentalization of Jaspers. Groups must formalize their consciousness since their essence is cooperation. A group's existence is impossible without an explicit awareness of the laws coordinating the thought and action of the individuals composing it. In short, the process of inserting individual significant structures into those of social classes means that every relatively autonomous element exists through its relation to other elements in a whole and that there is a necessary circle of relations between this whole and the elements and relations composing it. Such is the import of the *va-et-vient* process, which is at the base of the conceptual aspect of significant structure. Through this insertion process, in other words, significant structures come to be isolated.

This concept, then, becomes a hypothetical instrument for understanding .and explaining literary texts. While understanding implies the internal description of the relations making up a text's system, interpretation implies the genetic process of inserting it into a broader structure (a transindividual subject's pattern of mental categories). In this way, the text's meaning and historical specificity become functional, and the "why" of its formal and structural elements can be explained. These two aspects of the process are based on the epistemological inseparability of theory and praxis. A literary work is not born *ex nihilo*, nor is it an autonomous language system. Its structural coherence is dynamic and open, since there are constant centrifugal tensions created by its connotative richness. But this understanding of the text as a *process* cannot be reduced to a mere synchronic level without losing the text's historicity and meaning.[32] "It is beginning from the situation and from the necessity of a functional reply that one has coherence at the cultural level which is not mathematical," Goldmann says.[33] Contrary to static structuralism, a text's coherence is not logical, but functional.

Thus, the "why" of the text's organization is not immanent to the partial process of understanding it. It must be related to the world views demonstrable on the level of transindividual subjects. Here this "why" can find a response, at the homologous level of mental categories apparent in the theory and praxis of plural subjects. In the last analysis, it is by referring to the structuring process of world views that a work's aesthetic principle is intelligible. Goldmann writes, "Aesthetic value belongs to the social

---

32. Cf. *The Languages of Criticism*, p. 111, where Goldmann writes: "If we reserve the word 'structure' for mathematical structures, then I will have to find another for literary structures."

33. *Ibid.*, p. 114.

order; it is related to a transindividual logic."[34] Using Piaget, Goldmann's methodological question is, "Who is the subject? In whose life and practical activities did the mental structures, categories and the forms of thought and activity arise which determined the origin and behavior of the object studied?"[35] For "there is a division of labor and the problematic of literary history...is to situate human behavior in a framework within which it becomes necessary and comprehensible," Goldmann points out. As an introduction to the second category of his model, he concludes, "And I remind you that this is only possible at the level of a transindividual subject."[36]

Transindividual subject

With this concept, developed at length in "The Subject of Cultural Creation," Goldmann can begin to carry out a specifically sociological study of structures. Attempts to make structures functional, to interpret their significance and the factors of their transformation at the level of the individual alone, are simply inadequate. The structuring of the individual, one should recall, is explainable only with reference to his socialization, to the collective categories making up his becoming. Goldmann calls this level intrasubjective, the final insertion process involving the totality of plural subjects. It is at this level that history is created. In fact, it is through the collective subject that history becomes possible. At this level, too, there is an objective possibility of transformation that is methodologically comprehensible (see the chapter "Totality, Being and History" in Lukacs and Heidegger). The transindividual subject provides a unifying function between the mental categories of individuals and those structuring cultural creations. As Jacques Leenhardt has observed, "Thus, the theory of the 'subject' of cultural creation is complete and allows for the project of the sociology of literature...to be fully taken in because...Goldmann offers a totalizing grasp of cultural praxis as social praxis and so breaks with all anti-dialectical dualisms seeking to break and divide what is one."[37] This grasp is both

34. Ibid., p. 109.
35. Ibid., p. 99.
36. Ibid., p. 105.
37. Leenhardt, "A Propos de Marxisme et sciences humaines," Revue de l'institut de

critical and empirical, contrary to rationalist, positivist and existentialist conceptions of the subject, because the transindividual subject is comprehensive and describable within history. Indeed, by means of this concept and that of totality, the concept of world view is also given a concrete historical basis. Thus, the concept homology becomes rigorous, rather than merely symbolic or highly suggestive, as is the case with Lukacs, who ignored the dialectical potential of these categories. Through the collective subject one can explain the aggregate of mental categories forming the cultural bases upon which creative people produce their work. It is also this concept that accounts sociologically for the maximum dialectical comprehension of significant structures by not limiting them only to the level of consciousness. On the other hand, Goldmann is quick to add that no subject or cultural creation is purely social. By relating artistic works to a cultural sign system (or the mental categories of the collective consciousness), one is able to see them as specific within a more general cultural structure. Goldmann writes, "But I do not doubt the existence of the artist; I simply say that he does not invent his universe, that he creates it from the givens which are in society and which others have elaborated."[38]

Those who accuse Goldmann of eliminating the individual creative artist, genius or originality have grossly misread such categories as world view and possible consciousness. In *Recherches dialectiques,* for example, he writes, "Originality is certainly a *necessary* condition, but it is not *sufficient.*"[39] A few pages later, he adds, *"The more the work is the expression of a thinker or a writer of genius, the more it can be understood by itself*, without the need of the historian to have recourse to biography or the intentions of the creator. The strongest personality is that which best identifies with the life of the spirit, i.e., with the essential forces of social consciousness in its active and creative aspects." It is in this sense that he calls the literary work the meeting of the *"je"* and the *"nous,"*[40] the artist often expressing what is non-conscious in the latter. The fact is,

sociologie, 3-4 (1973), p. 560.

38. "Pensée dialectique et sujet transindividuel," *Bulletin de la société française de philosophie,* 3 (July-September 1970), p. 115. The entire discussion section is pertinent here.

39. *Recherches dialectiques,* pp. 31ff.

40. *The Languages of Criticism,* p. 334.

Goldmann's model adopts neither Lukacs' 19th-century theory of realism nor the complete negative critique so evident in Adorno's *Théorie esthétique* (see "The Topicality of the Question of the Subject" in *Lukacs and Heidegger* for Goldmann's views on Adorno). In this way, he has constructed a uniquely usable model.

Totality

As early as his thesis on Kant, published in 1945, Goldmann was concerned with the concept of totality, primarily because of his discovery of Lukacs' *History and Class Consciousness*, but also because of his study of Hegel, Marx and Pascal. In his book on Kant he writes, "The reader who has followed thus far will no doubt have realized that *totality* in its two principal forms, the *universe* and the *human community*, constitutes for me the most important philosophical category, as much in the field of epistemology as in ethics or aesthetics."[41] While the concept of significant structure underlies the other concepts of his model, the concept of totality provides its macro-analytical overview. By describing it as the dynamic interaction of the classes and groups composing society in a given historical period, Goldmann positions this category in the world rather than outside it, as are Kant's thing-in-itself and Hegel's Absolute Spirit. Thus, Goldmann's frequent repetition of the dictum that the history of the problem is the problem of history explains the scope required by his *genetic* structuralism and provided, in turn, by totality. Through it, history is seen as a unified, knowable and social process. Its very comprehensiveness allows one to carry out both a positive (descriptive) and a critical (interpretive) analysis. Like the insertion process mentioned earlier, totality, too, is based on Piaget's interactionist theory. Since society is made up of relative totalities in constant interaction, one can never consider any society (as a totality) as given. Goldmann explains this in *Kierkegaard Vivant*, relying upon Piagetian terminology to avoid all suggestions of idealism: "Now, if man's behavior is always the creation of coherent structures or relative totalities, it thus represents the destruction of totalities because it is historical and because every creation of a new totality is a destruction, a transformation of previous structures. There is only totalization to the

---

41. *Immanuel Kant* (New Left Books: London, 1971), p. 50.

extent that there is detotalization."[42] And later, "We cannot even comprehend it (totality) as something which is approximative, but only as a process which we are gradually producing. The discussion around this problem has gone so far that Piaget decided to speak no longer of structures but rather of destructuration."[43]

The totality is reflected in the praxis of the classes that mediate it, and through the latter, literary works can be understood in their dialectical concreteness. Pertinent here are the three remaining categories of Goldmann's model: world view, possible consciousness-objective possibility and homology. On the one hand, totality refers to the entire socio-historical process and offers a critical level of interpretation with respect to the partial ideological perspectives of plural subjects. On the other hand, world view describes a particular group's projection of this totality as an effort to respond to the problems posed to it by other groups and by the natural environment. The world view of a particular group, then, is nothing other than its implicit attempt to order all of society, in which one can read out the projection of the group's maximum possibilities. It is in this extrapolation that one can analyze the point of balance and coherence achieved by individuals in their group context. Goldmann writes in *Lukacs and Heidegger,* "Coherence linked to function is constituted at the level of mental structures starting from a given historical situation and in the perspective of a determinate praxis of a group in relation to other groups."[44] This ordering of its relations in society at the global level is required for a transindividual subject's survival at the practical level. (Gramsci's term for it is hegemony.) Thus, the status of totality is not an abstract and metaphysical one as it is for Dilthey and even for Lukacs, to some extent. Goldmann writes, "It is the very principle of totality that affirms precisely that there is no such thing as a theory that does not derive from facts. . .and there is no fact that can be seen outside of an explicit, conscious, or implicit world view."[45]

42. *Kierkegaard vivant* (Gallimard: Paris, 1966), pp. 267-268.
43. *Ibid.,* p. 272.
44. *Lukacs and Heidegger,* p. 85.
45. "Revolution et bureaucratie," *L'Homme et la société,* 21 (July-September 1971), p. 77.

World view

World views are eminently concrete, positive and dialectical. Contrary to their being based on psychological types à la Dilthey, moreover, Goldmann bases them on plural subjects. At this sociological leve, the individual level can be surpassed, though not erased. The inverse is not true, however, for the individual level has no totalizing potential capable of being extended to the entire society. The concept of world view, which Jean Duvignaud called Goldmann's greatest contribution, explains the documentary level of a literary work and, in so doing, distinguishes the particular task of any aesthetics having sociological aspirations.

The transindividuality of a world view explains the unity of a text or system of texts, its system of categories and values. As Mukarovsky confirms, "The world view, which is manifested as the noetic base or as ideology or as a philosophical system, exists not only outside the work of art as something expressed by it, but becomes the very principle of its artistic structuration and acts upon the reciprocal relations between its components and the global meaning of the artistic sign."[47] Contrary to a certain Marxist and semiological perspective in which a world view is seen as the ideology or false consciousness of a given group, however, Goldmann is quite explicit in guarding against the implications in such a perspective. World views (whether virtual in social groups or explicit in literary texts) are not mere "appearances" of another structural level, in which case they would be purely passive reflections. They have an action function, as Gramsci would say. That is, the elaboration of a world view renders the common sense of the subaltern classes rational, critical, systematic and unitary. In this sense, Goldmann and Gramsci are very close in emphasizing the importance of the superstructural level as real. In fact, Gramsci's notion of common sense is similar to Goldmann's real consciousness, and his notion of world view similar to Goldmann's same category.[48]

At this point, one should say that the literary work's relation to

46. Duvignaud, "Goldmann et la 'Vision du Monde'," *Revue de l'institut de sociologie*, 3-4 (1973), p. 554.

47. *Il Significato dell'Estetica*, p. 462.

48. See Gramsci, *Quaderni del Carcere,* especially "Il Materialismo Storico e la Filosofia di Benedetto Croce" (Einaudi: Milan, 1975).

a given social group, or an aggregate of them, is a privileged and critical one for Goldman. It is privileged insofar as the writer, at an extremely advanced level of coherence, is among the first to constitute "the aggregate of categories tending towards coherent structures, aggregates proper to certain privileged social groups whose thought, sensibility and behavior are oriented toward a global organization of interhuman relations and relations between man and nature."[49] The literary work is critical insofar as it displays the author's creativity and originality in his relation to society. Depending upon this relation at a given moment, the writer is caught between the need to deform and to organize, to remember and to forget in relation to the cultural system from which he takes his language. Nor is Goldmann talking about the content of works here but is referring to their structural organization as being homologous to the pattern of a plural subject's mental categories. The contents of various texts can be very different but still be informed by the same world view. Indeed, Goldmann unfailingly goes beyond the monographical approach to study an author's total *opera*.[50]

As is apparent in "Sociological and Cultural Denunciation" and "Genetic Structuralism and Stylistic Analysis," Goldmann also tried to set up micro-analytical correspondences between the text's structure and the literary means used to create it, which would carry over to the level of world view.[51] This level concerns the relationship between the text's unity and its richness but also the determining importance of the signified over the signifier and of significant global structures over partial ones. This coherence involves linguistic forms and style, an area in which the contemporary semiological research of Lotman and Uspenskij is most relevant in making Goldmann's model more rigorous. As Goldmann says, "I wanted to show that it was possible to bring together abstract linguistic or stylistic forms with what I have chosen to call the form of content."[52]

49. "Jean Piaget and Philosophy," p. 158.

50. According to Italian semiologist Maria Corti, Goldmann's method is much more fruitful when it relates social structures to the structures of a large literary system. "It is the literary whole, then, that brings into relief the more social aspect of the message." *Principi della Communicazione Letteraria* (Bompiani: Milan, 1976), p. 28.

51. See also the essays on micro-structures in Jean Genet's *The Blacks* and in various poems, now collected in Goldmann's *Structures mentales et création culturelle* (Anthropos: Paris, 1970).

52. *The Language of Criticism*, p. 108.

To conclude the discussion of this category, it should be said that the influence on Goldmann of Bernard Groethysen's work *Origines de l'ésprit bourgeois en France* (Gallimard, 1927), wherein the category of world view is used to great effect, has been unfortunately overlooked. Goldmann clearly relied upon this book for his own study *The Philosophy of the Enlighten-ment.*[53] Although he most likely got the category more directly from Lukacs' *The Soul and the Forms*, he recognized the latter's idealistic use of it.[54] In fact, in *The Hidden God* he describes Lukacs' tragic world view as Kantian, i.e., without an intrinsic connection to history.[55]

Possible consciousness-objective possibility

Since groups always depend on other groups for their own status, and since this relationship is constantly changing, they seldom achieve a highly coherent self-understanding of their relations within the total process of society.[56] That is why Goldmann describes their theoretical praxis as largely non-conscious. The structuring of a group's mental categories is generally latent or virtual. In *History and Class Consciousness*, from which Goldmann takes the next categories of his model — namely, possible consciousness-objective possibility — Lukacs writes, "Regarded abstractly and formally, then, class consciousness implies a class-conditioned *unconsciousness* of one's own socio-historical and economic condition."[57] He continues, "This condition is given as a definite structural relation, a definite formal nexus which appears to govern the whole of life." Within the immediate activity of the individuals making up a class, though, this structural relation is usually ignored. The individual's use of certain categories generally takes place at a practical and non-reflective level. This rich and multiform level of individual consciousness, often highly subjective and pressed in

---

53. Goldmann's book was published in English by Routledge & Kegan Paul, London, 1973. With regard to Groethysen, see "Trois penseurs sans ideologie," *Cause commune*, 6 (April 1973), pp. 9-20.

54. *Recherches dialectiques*, pp. 33, 41, 42, 254-255.

55. *The Hidden God*, p. 22.

56. See "Le Concept de conscience possible pour la communication," *La Creation culturelle dans la société moderne* (Denoel Gonthier: Paris, 1971), p. 20. Goldmann relies on Piaget's interactionist epistemology here to explain the validity of these concepts.

57. *History and Class Consciousness* (MIT Press: Cambridge, Mass., 1971), p. 52.

by the urgencies of the moment, Goldmann calls real (actual) consciousness.[58] To the extent that individuals within a given class remain unaware of the structural relations within and between their class and others, the world view of that class will remain opaque and virtual.

From this viewpoint, the artist is in the vanguard of those individuals making up a transindividual subject. Far from succumbing to the overwhelming manifold of everyday life, as do those who remain at the level of real consciousness, the artist objectifies it. That is, he constructs a possible vision inherent in the mental categories of a transindividual subject with which he identifies, whether intentionally or not. By carrying certain values to their maximum possible consciousness, he in a sense creates them, through the logic of metaphor and the laws of narration. But while the articulation of a world view is a critical act of the artist, he does not create it *ex nihilo*. Even the expression of his private impulses or the voicing of general human needs through fantastic or utopian perspectives is historically determinate and necessarily related to some dominant reality, perhaps in need of being transcended in order for him to declare a transhistorical vision ignored by his contemporaries.[59] In other words, from the perspective of possible consciousness, no world view can be separated from social praxis, i.e., from the category of objective possibility. The price one pays for such a separation is an arbitrary epistemological dualism. No consciousness speaks from outside the totality, as Adorno would have it by postulating the critical consciousness, or Husserl the transcendental ego. The artist can begin to imagine a vision of society only from within it. Thus, he is determined as much as he determines and reveals his epoch in the very act of transcending the immediacy around him. The flight of the artist's vision is defined by the objective possibility of his position within a given culture.

Since it is transindividual subjects who create history, generate world views and make change possible, it is by understanding the

58. See "Conscience réele et conscience possible, conscience adequate et fause conscience," *Marxisme et sciences humaines,* p. 126.

59. See Albert Memmi, "Problèmes de la sociologie de la littérature," in Georges Gurvitch, ed., *Traite de Sociologie,* vol. 2 (P.U.F.: Paris, 1963), pp. 299-314. Memmi writes, "One too often forgets, finally...that the sociology of literature must also be a *sociology of fantasy.* We have proposed elsewhere a *sociology of desire* which could perhaps be related to what Goldmann calls *consciousness of the possible,*" p. 306.

structural tendencies of such subjects that one can estimate the field of choices and the categorial horizon of the artist. This is so because the mental categories he elaborates and the sign system upon which he relies and by which he is structured are virtually present in the real consciousness of his contemporaries. On the other hand, it is pre-eminently the artist who leaves the immediate subjective level of real consciousness by bringing into consciousness the structural and global tendencies of a social class. This is Goldmann's understanding of *poesis*.

As an archaeologist, then, the artist objectifies and exposes the relationships of which most individuals are unaware by going beyond the subjective and individual, by carrying these relationships to their conclusion. Lukacs writes, "The objective theory of class consciousness is the theory of its objective possibility."[60] In other words, it is from the perspective of a relative totality that the artist is able to distance himself from the real consciousness of individuals and arrive at the objective possibility and possible consciousness of their tendencies. "By relating consciousness to the whole of society, it becomes possible to infer the thoughts and feelings which men would have in a particular situation if they were *able* to assess both it and the interests arising from it in their impact on immediate action and on the whole structure of society," Lukacs writes.[61] The writer follows the thread to its source; he traces the mental categories structuring individuals to their genesis in social praxis. In doing so, he uncovers the structural tendencies of these "hidden" categories apparent only in the dynamic whole of the relations of those plural subjects composing society. In portraying the drama of his characters, the writer necessarily takes note of class situations that make certain actions and ideas possible for those individuals within them. By elaborating the world views of plural subjects, he can also determine the thinkability or unthinkability of certain projects on the level of the non-conscious consciousness of individuals within those plural subjects. The objective possibility of an individual, then, is composed of two factors: his external situation (the aggregate of social relations making up the plural subject to which the individual belongs) and his mental categories

---

60. *History and Class Consciousness*, p. 79.
61. *Ibid.*, p. 51.

(also determining the limits of his action and the horizon of his vision, the possible consciousness of the social class to which he belongs).[62]

Goldmann writes, "The problem is, then, not that of knowing what a group is thinking, but of knowing what changes are capable of being produced in its consciousness without there being a change in the essential nature of the group."[63] One can study significant structures by determining to what extent the activity of individuals within a given class remains functional without there being a qualitative change in their social status or their world view. By knowing the aggregate of the relationships of a given class, one can outline the limits of its structural possibilities. As Lukacs writes: "The essence of history lies precisely in the changes undergone by those *structural forms* which are the focal points of man's interaction with the environment at any given moment and which determine the objective nature of both his inner and outer life. But this only becomes objectively possible (and hence can only be adequately comprehended) when the individuality...of an epoch or an historical figure, etc., is grounded in the character of these structural forms, when it is discovered and exhibited in them and through them."[64]

Both of these categories under discussion, of course, must also be placed within the base category of significant structure to secure the anthropological homogeneity of Goldmann's model. With these categories Goldmann requires one to go beyond literature toward broader structures in order to understand the historical transformations of literary structures themselves.[65] In this light, the history of literature is neither the mere sequence of literary facts, a chronology of texts implying some sort of autonomous evolution between them, nor simply another occasion to represent the history of a more important reality behind it. Both extremes are reductive and are based on an often unwitting epistemological dualism.

62. See "Objective Possibility and Possible Consciousness," *Lukács and Heidegger*, pp. 51-66.
63. *La création culturelle dans la société moderne*, p. 10. On p. 59, he calls this category basic for the comprehension of human history.
64. *History and Class Consciousness*, p. 153.
65. See "The Social Structure and the Collective Consciousness of Structures," p. 40.

Homology

With the concept of homology, which completes his model, Goldmann intends to make the art-society relationship into a paradigm, i.e., to conceptualize the passage from one level to the other. By declaring the interdependence of theory and praxis, one is committed to the success of spelling out such a passage. Still, this success is not apparent in *Toward a Sociology of the Novel*, for which Goldmann is accused of literary determinism because of his description of a homology between the *nouveau roman* and contemporary capitalist society. One must keep in mind his own cautionary note, however, that the seeming disappearance of active mediations between the artist and contemporary reified society is an inductive rather than an *a priori* conclusion.[66] By homology, Goldmann does not mean that the literary work is reduced to the level of imitation. One should recall that any application of the category must take into account the level of possible consciousness. Furthermore, the interdependence of these two different levels is structural. It is not a matter of relating directly the content of a literary work to the historical facts outside it.[67] Instead, it is a question of relating the collective consciousness of a social class, or classes, to the imaginary structure of a literary work.

Lotman and Uspenskij have used homology in much the same way as Goldmann.[68] In fact, they establish morphological homologies between art (defined as a secondary modeling system) and its object. Any recodification offered by the literary model pre-exists in the semiological system used by individual writers. At the risk of simplifying their argument, they point out that any semiological sign system is a social product and language, in turn, answers to a semiological system. Art, as a linguistic subsystem of culture, is built on a code that selects the events which will be translated into elements of literary texts. These latter, then, are realizations of potentialities inherent in a culture. As an organizing mechanism based on language, culture generates structurality, and, in so doing, creates a social sphere

---

66. *Toward a Sociology of the Novel*, pp. 10-12.
67. *Littérature et société*, p. 203.
68. *Semiotica e cultura*, the introduction by D. Ferrari-Bravo and chapters 1 and 3. "Tesi sull' 'Arte come sistema secondario di modellizzazione'," and "Sul meccanismo semiotico della cultura."

around man. Language, in particular, gives members of the collectivity the sense of structurality and, in this way, individuals are obliged to treat phenomena as structures. Of course, this is just a glimpse into the complex but highly convincing thought of Lotman and Uspenskij. Undoubtedly, their observations reinforce Goldmann's use of homology, his most criticized concept, and point the way to a more rigorous application of it.

Rossi-Landi is another semiologist who uses this category to describe the relationship between linguistic production and material production. Although he is directly indebted to Goldmann for this category, he gives it a semiological perspective.[69] According to Rossi-Landi, both types of production are human artifacts and at the basis of these two orders there is a common anthropogenic root verified ontogenetically and philogenetically. To accept this, one need only accept the total indissoluble unity between man and all of his productions. To separate them, he says, is too simplistic and inexact. What is more, by doing so, one is faced with an asymmetrical conjunction of inexplicably heterogeneous elements — similar to the perverse ontological dualism between the body and soul. There are, however, four interconnected points which demonstrate a homology between the two orders of production: (1) man produces the two orders simultaneously, i.e., one never exists without the other; (2) these two orders (*homo loquens* and *homo faber*) form the basis on which man is social and distinct from animals; (3) linguistic communication presupposes a world of real objects to which discourse refers — language gives one the ability to distinguish and manipulate objects in a system of the division of labor; (4) the social operations that govern the two orders of production are largely identical — a growing child undergoes the product systems of both orders.

Even at the risk of confusing the reader, I have presented this new research to indicate the importance of this category, both for Goldmann's model and for any sociology or semiology of culture that claims to be scientifically rigorous. Goldmann himself gives less explicit theoretical attention to this concept than to the

---

69. Ferruccio Rossi-Landi, *Il Linguaggio come Lavoro e come Mercato* (Bompiani: Milan, 1968), pp. 150-156.

others, although it is in accord with them. In *Toward a Sociology of the Novel*, Goldmann writes, "the relations between the truly important work and the social group, which — through the medium of the creator — *is, in the last resort,* the true subject of creation, are of the same order of relations between the elements of the work and the work as a whole."[70] It is this statement which has brought a good deal of criticism against him,[71] mostly because Goldmann failed to give it enough of a theoretical definition. In *Le Littérature et le social*, perplexity over this concept is nearly unanimous. These critics suggest that perhaps homology means parellelism, superimposition, juxtaposition, emanation, converging action, reciprocity or analogy.

On the basis of his acquaintance with Goldmann's other categories, however, the reader should now have a clear framework for describing the theoretical role of homology. If one begins with its controversial use in *Toward a Sociology of the Novel*, he finds that it means a "necessary" and "intelligible" relation.[72] In *Littérature et société*, Goldmann substitutes the word "correspondence" and "strict bond" for it.[73] In other words, homology has nothing to do with the arbitrariness of a relationship between a literary work and society that is implied by the concepts of juxtaposition or parallelism. Generally, these pertain to a formalistic method of ideal types. What is lacking in such a method is what lies at the heart of Goldmann's genetic structuralism: dialectics. It has already been pointed out how Goldmann avoids a relationship of identity between the two levels. And, by recalling the complex use Goldmann makes of world view and possible consciousness, the reader should also recognize the error of regarding homology in a determinist or emanationist fashion. The notion of superimposition, of course, is cancelled with the same stroke.

If Goldmann provides no further direct clues as to the nature of the homologous "necessity" between the world view of a social group and the structure of the literary work, one need only define

---

70. *Toward a Sociology of the Novel*, p. 158.
71. See Stefan Morawski, *L'Absolu et la forme* (Edition Klinsieck: Paris, 1972), pp. 200, 204-205, 209. See also the criticism of C. Bouazis in R. Escarpit, ed., *Le Littéraire et le social* (Flammarion: Paris, 1970). The articles of Mury, Orrecchioni and Dubois are also relevant.
72. *Toward a Sociology of the Novel*, pp. 158-159.
73. *Littérature et société*, p. 204.

it in terms of the other categories of his model. In this way, one discovers that it is a dialectical constructivist principle involving a functional necessity. As Goldmann once explained, the structural coherence of the literary work (the level of its comprehension) has a *functional* coherence within a broader structure (the level of explanation and insertion). The two levels of coherence are revealed through a single *va-et-vient* methodological process.[74] As is evident, Goldmann relies upon the interactionist epistemology of Piaget, which he used to define the concept of significant structure. Homology, then, must be seen from the perspective of this latter category. "It (homology) is, therefore, a question of the relation between a structure and a function," Goldmann says.[75] It is an operational category describing the methodically constructed relation resulting from the comprehension-explanation process applied to the literary work by genetic structuralism. The very circularity of this process of *va-et-vient* constructs the homologous relationship while outlining the broader structure of homology that "the hypothesis of its existence at the scientific level constitutes a highly operatory instrument both for the study of the work and the collective consciousness, since the structural exploration of each of them allows one to discover certain elements of the other which had escaped direct observation and the immanent study."[76] If homology is a methodological hypothesis, its cogency nonetheless derives from a distinct anthropological and philosophical position taken primarily from Piaget and Lukacs.

From the perspective of totality, for example, it is impossible to presume that homology describes a deterministic, univocal or immediate relation of facts on different levels. Contrary to a positivistic viewpoint, which regards the world simply as an aggregate of individual data that are automatically significant, the perspective of totality sees facts as the result of relations. That is, they are constructions that must be studied in their dynamic structuring processes. Homology is far from being a mere nominalistic exercise based on a researcher's intuition. The whole is not reducible to the sum of its parts but is the distinct outcome of

74. *Critique sociologique et critique psychanalytique* (Editions de l'institut de sociologie: Brussels, 1965), p. 233.

75. *Ibid.*

76. *Littérature et société*, p. 204.

their relations. Society is such a whole and, to understand the literary work, one cannot isolate it as a monadic element outside its context. It, too, is a construction within society, and the need to see its functional relatedness within larger structures is the very description of the hypothesis of homology. Such is Goldmann's anthropological view of art. As part of the theoretical realm, a literary work is homologous to the collective consciousness of a class, or classes, if for no other reason than that of the essential relatedness of theory and praxis and the need to see individuals and their creations within the totality of their multi-leveled relations. Lotman would call this totality a sign system, or a culture. Goldmann explains further, in *Structures mentales et créations culturelles,* that homology pertains not only to the level of conscious ideology, but also to the *non-conscious* level of the work's imaginary universe and of the collective consciousness of a group within the totality.[77]

The concept of coherence, of course, differs for the structure of the literary work and for the structure of a group's mental categories, even if these two levels are homologous. Goldmann has no intention of resolving the literary work's polysemism into a mono-signification, although knowledge of a work inevitably presupposes its reduction to the level of abstract language. On the contrary, he merely wishes to circumscribe the horizon within which this polysemism is functionally significant. Goldmann respects the work's own inner dialectical requirements. Indeed, he begins by analyzing the work's inner aesthetic formation, wherein its *littérairité* and intransitivity can be grasped, before passing to its functionalization within a broader structure. By doing so, he avoids reducing it to its genesis and can also determine its negative critique and the distance the artist achieves from the real consciousness of individuals. Thus, the dialectical aspect of homology is borne out insofar as the correspondence is constructed across the categories of possible consciousness and objective possibility. Expressed this way, the homologous relation can also demonstrate a surpassing of the given reality, a relation to transhistorical values that often are represented only by way of their absence.[78] According to

---

77. *Structures mentales et création culturelle,* p. 394.
78. *Littérature et société,* p. 206. Goldmann writes: "As for negativity and the

Goldmann, negativity and an element of transcendence are necessary to every great work, even if their very expression is specified by the historical situation demanding them, and even if the artist's very self-expression is circumscribed by his objective possibility traceable in the limits of his social relationships.

These, then, are the six categories making up Goldmann's model. The process of having theoretically ordered them should both clear up the confusion over Goldmann's particular indebtedness to his mentors and provide the systematic view of them which he had promised his public.

William Q. Boelhower

---

aspiration to a *dépassement*, it seems to us that they are basic in every literary creation to the extent that. . . by tending to realize a coherent structure or, more precisely, to push a process of structuration to its extreme limits, literary works must necessarily find themselves in conflict with existing structures and be formulated in relation to them and to the factors of destructuration."

1. Subject and Object in the Human Sciences

I would like to begin this lecture by thanking my friend Lotringer for this chance to speak to you today.... Given the nature of this lecture cycle, I will speak to you about methodological and epistemological issues, particularly as they are related to the human sciences.

The dominant theme of current discussion, the one that demands most attention, concerns the subject-object relationship. It has become increasingly clear that no human fact can be either understood or explained when taken from its context. Furthermore, for those who are not followers of what I call the ideology of structuralism of linguistic inspiration, this context is not only an intellectual one. It is also social, economic and even political. This is the basic idea behind the creation of the sociology of knowledge.

Once within this perspective, one meets up with the crucial problem that Hegel brought to light a century ago and which is at the center of Marx's thought as well. Society is more than an object of study external to the researcher. He himself belongs to it. The entire categorical structure of his consciousness and his emotions are social facts and are responsible to the same scientific study. The subject, then, is part of the object studied. The object can be found within the subject's consciousness. Hegel called this the subject-object identity, which evolves during the course of history and which must be specified and defined anew with each

---

1. Goldmann, "Sujet et objet en sciences humaines," *Raison Présente,* 7 (January-March 1971), pp. 83-101. This text was only partially edited by Goldmann. His wife completed the task. It was originally a talk given in May 1969 at the Sorbonne as part of a colloquium on "Nouveaux courants de la Critique."

research project. This is quite an important datum of the human sciences, according to which the nature of objectivity is seen in an essentially different way than it is in the natural sciences.

On this basis, I would like to outline briefly the area that my lecture will cover and the principles that I define myself by, indicating in this way what I do and do not accept. Obviously, my preliminary remarks still prove nothing as to the validity of the position that I defend and those that I criticize. I will continue to elaborate on this point throughout the lecture. Now, I would like to specify, as best I can, from where within society and intellectual life I and the other participants in this discussion speak. In short, what is the social and intellectual context of this discussion? First of all, there is the problem of genesis and synchrony. Lotringer has pointed out correctly that for some time now non-genetic structuralists have attempted to introduce history, or at least the concept of transformation, into their perspective. Although I have not closely followed the literature on this attempt, one need only read Foucault's latest book to see that, in spite of the rest, he does give the problem some attention. All the same, the contrasts over the concept of the subject are just as radical as before. Without this concept, though, it seems impossible to deal scientifically with the problem of transformation.

It was above all with reference to non-genetic structuralism (especially when influenced by linguistics) that I chose the title of this lecture, which involves the alternatives of continuity and discontinuity and the subject and the object. I do not grant such radical dualities any scientific status, though, since they only belong to a host of pseudo-alternatives or pseudo-dualities, all having the same epistemological status. Unfortunately, due to the lack of time, I cannot elaborate them now. I will mention only the following: structure-process, fact-value, subjectivity-objectivity, comprehension-explanation and determinism-freedom.

Opposition to non-genetic structuralism, however, does not seem sufficient for defining the field in which current dialectical thought is affirmed. For this reason, I will turn back for a moment to recall that during the last 20 years this thought has first had to assert itself against Sartre's existentialism and only then against the non-genetic and anti-historical structuralism of

Levi-Strauss, Foucault, Greimas, Althusser and Barthes. After all, these two "isms" are both complementary and unilateral. Each defends one of the false alternatives or pseudo-dualities that I have enumerated. One emphasizes the subject, freedom, the project, values, process and comprehension; the other, structure, facts, objects, discontinuity and necessity.

As a sociologist, I refuse to discuss ideas abstractly, torn from their context.... For quite some time I have had to struggle against Sartrean existentialism, which once appeared unchallengeable to most students. This involved defending the concept of the object and that of structure insofar as they exist within the free subject. I have stressed how important it is to have a notion of discontinuity, but not at the expense of continuity. Otherwise, genesis and history must be excluded. Then I defended the objective and real foundation of subjectivity as well as the importance of human and social reality in founding values, that is, they need to be based on facts. Against a new generation of students, I must now speak up for the existence of the subject and praxis in human and social reality. I must point out continuity in discontinuity, freedom in determinism, the presence of values in the establishing of facts, and so on. Why is it that what was evident yesterday now no longer exists? Why is it that what was so difficult to integrate into one's thought a few years ago is now not only real but seems to be the one and only aspect of reality? In short, what were the historical and social reasons behind the growth of existentialist thought in Europe from 1912 to around 1950 and even 1960? And what are the historical and social reasons behind the contemporary development of the opposite perspective, non-genetic structuralism?

I am inclined to choose 1911 as the year in which the first public manifestation of existentialism in Western Europe occurred. It was then that Lukacs' *The Soul and the Forms* appeared, with a chapter on Kierkegaard and another on tragedy, on man's limits and the limit *par excellence*: death. Later on, as you know, Jaspers and Heidegger became the great German existentialists (the latter greatly influenced by Lukacs) and Sartre the French exponent. In 1917 Lukacs began to turn toward Marxism. The end of the growth and influence of existentialism seems more difficult to pinpoint. This occurred nevertheless after World War II; in France, probably around 1954, with the 20th Congress of the Communist Party in the U.S.S.R., and above all in 1962, with the end of the Algerian war. But if these two events deeply disturbed the existentialist influence, it is because this thought was already in decline and had lost its social base. In fact, existentialism began to fade with the development of the mechanisms of economic self-regulation and with the establishment of a technocratic society and organized capitalism.

In other words, the history of existentialist philosophy quite precisely corresponds with what I call the crisis period of capitalism. This crisis was due to the rise of monopolies and trusts that brought about the destruction of the regulatory role of the free market. Furthermore, a planned economy with governmental intervention appeared only after World War II.

Without going into details that exceed the aim of the present lecture, I will simply mention the constant succession of economic, social and political crises from 1914 to 1945, following upon a long period of relative calm in Western Europe throughout the 19th century. From 1914 to 1918, World War I. From 1918 to 1923, the social and political crises, especially in Germany. From 1929 to 1933, the most severe economic crisis that the Western world has known. Then, national socialism and World War II.

Let us now consider non-genetic structuralism, which seems rather difficult to understand outside of the social context in which it developed. At least in France, this movement took the baton from existentialism. The common element among the various forms of non-genetic structuralism is the negation of the subject and man's role in changing history. It seems closely related to the transitional forms that modern society assumed with the creation of the self-regulatory mechanisms. Most likely, these forms constitute the passage from the crisis of capitalism during the first half of the 20th century and future social forms. Sociologists have called this social structure "technocratic society" and "organized capitalism." Here decisions are put more and more into the hands of a relatively restricted social class, which I will call the "technocrats." At least for a while, this class has successfully won the consensus of the great majority of traditional workers (technicians and trained personnel) by assuring them higher salaries and more leisure. During this period, sociologists greatly differing from each other elaborated theories about a totally integrated and acritical society: Raymond Aron and Daniel Bell both developed a theory about the end of ideology; David Riesman affirmed the disappearance in man of interior radar; Herbert Marcuse announced the birth of one-dimensional man. On the philosophical and methodological level, the reality of the subject was denied and man's significance was negated.

Throughout the existentialist period, it was necessary to insist on the fact that the subject is not completely free. He is limited not only by external possibilities, but also by the fact that the world is present in the very structuring of his thought and emotions. (As we will see, this is so even beyond the fact that the subject is never himself and is rarely individual.) With respect to linguistically derived structuralism, it is equally important for us to insist that there is always a subject. One cannot simply imagine that structures effect transformations, through a mere internal process of change. There are subjects and it is they who make history, i.e., transform structures.

It is within the context of this debate and this intellectual space that I will now try to speak about the fundamental methodological principles of the human sciences.

I could have spoken about method in the sociology of literature. I would, however, like to stress that in this domain method is only one part of the more general problematic of the human sciences. Whether one studies history, philosophy, the history of the sciences, literary history or sociology, the problems are the same. Furthermore, there is one level, that of studying and understanding empirical facts. I consider it very important to remind this assembly of students that, when faced with the variety of methods that will be proposed during this lecture cycle, one should not make a choice on the basis of personal aspirations or preferences. One should choose the one that best allows him to understand human facts, the facts he is studying. Method is always a technique, a strategy for understanding realities. When speaking about method in the social sciences, I believe that one should raise certain questions. For example, one should question the value of positivist sociology, which has dedicated many resources, investigations and monographs to the analysis of French society without, however, being able to foresee in April 1968 the possibility of the crisis that occurred in May. This poses a methodological problem and it is at this level that I will attempt to explain genetic structuralism alongside the alternatives I have stated above and their correspondences with existentialism, non-genetic structuralism and positivism.

The first basic principle of genetic structuralism is that human facts (whatever they may be: Pascal's *Pensées*, the French Revolution, the crusades) must be related to the behavior of a subject in order to be understood. We will soon consider the nature of this subject, but it is obvious that human facts are the result of human behavior and can be very precisely defined. Man transforms the world around him in order to achieve a better balance between himself (as subject) and the world. One writes a book, makes a road or builds a house to change the world. Now, all human behavior is meaningful and makes sense; whether the subject is within a situation or related to another subject, his action is functional. As you see, we have two crucial categories in the human sciences: structure and function. A function is what allows one to better his equilibrium. And, in order to get rid of a basic prejudice of the traditional human sciences, it should immediately be added that this functionality, this meaning, is not necessarily conscious. Even if the action of a cat in catching a mouse is unconscious, this does not mean that his behavior is therefore meaningless. It can still be translated into the language of problem (hunger) and solution (the act of catching the mouse). On the other hand, human facts are always related to consciousness but are not *per se* adequate. This means that if, for example, I study a literary work as a significant structure, the latter is not necessarily the one that the writer wanted or of which he was aware. I am interested in studying human facts as significant structures. Human behavior is made up of different elements that pass through one's consciousness and, in relation to a social group, their function is to improve one's relationship with the world.

I can now define the concept of the subject and raise the main issue: *what subject?* The concept of the subject that non-genetic structuralists criticize is the subject as individual. It is true that the human sciences are increasingly demonstrating that the subject of human behavior and the creator of structures could not be an individual. After brief reflection this is obvious. Except for the libido, human behavior goes beyond the individual subject. Pretend that a very heavy stone must be lifted and that there are three people to do it. It is impossible to understand this action on the basis of the ego, the *pour soi* or the organic subject, as Descartes and even Sartre wanted to do. (Although each of these terms has its peculiar meaning, they all indicate an individual subject.) It is not true that the stone is lifted by, let us say, John, Peter, or Andrew; nor even by the sum of them. We term the subject that group of individuals by which an action and a result can be understood. Now, it is a proven fact that all historical actions, from hunting and farming to aesthetic and cultural creation, can only be studied scientifically, can only be understood and made rational when they are related to collective subjects. Of course, such subjects are not permanently fixed. The three individuals involved in lifting the stone are not the same as those who, let us say, built this house. In a given epoch and at a given moment, there are innumerable groups that perform thousands of actions. Among these, certain groups are particularly important because their actions and behavior tend to structure society as a whole. They also structure human relationships and man's rapport with nature. These groups are privileged because they tend to act not on partial elements of a social structure (Parisian physicians, for example), but on the global human universe. Marx called these privileged groups social classes. One should see if there are still others which have a decisive role in history, bring about historical change and, in any case, have a dominant influence in major cultural creations. It is an empirical problem.

Cultural works are great to the extent that they express a global image of man and the universe. In studying such important works, one should investigate privileged groups and the global structure of society. It is through such groups that we can comprehend the genesis of a work. Obviously, thousands of people make up these groups and perform thousands of actions. (The social group does not exist beyond the people who compose it.) When the members of a group are all motivated by the same situation and have the same orientation, they elaborate functional mental structures for themselves as a group within their historical situation. One cannot have mental structures for each separate action. These mental structures, then, have an active role in history and are also expressed in major philosophical, artistic and literary creations.

That is why the entire problematic of a scientific sociology (I say this parenthetically) is not that of surveying what people are now thinking, even if this can yield very exact, photographic information on what they will do the day after tomorrow. Rather, one must isolate the fundamental process of the historical transformation of structures. It is men, groups and social classes that elaborate structures oriented toward providing them with equilibrium. And, of course, when such structures are no longer functional, they elaborate new ones. The essential task of sociology is to discover the transforming elements of the old structure before they have become manifest, to seek what is virtual in it.

As a methodological example, let us take the sociology of Parsons, who claims to be a functionalist-structuralist in contrast to the non-functionalist structuralism developed in France. Parsons considers functions only in relation to a given structure. Whatever fails to maintain this structure is "dysfunctional." To me, the latter term is meaningless. What sociology calls "dysfunctional" in an existing structure, in an existing form of thought or society, is obviously functional with respect to evolving elements in them, elements in the process of being born. If forms of dysfunctionality appear, this is because existing thought and behavior no longer correspond to a society in transformation. Men are creating a new rationality, a new structure that will be functional. At this point, human phenomena are dysfunctional with respect to the past and functional with respect to the future.

The first important methodological step is to isolate the important objects and then to study their meaning, i.e., their functional relations with a subject, which, ultimately, is always collective.

We have no scientific means to study the necessary relation between Racine's plays and his consciousness. I have no way of knowing if a certain young lady will get married within the next two years, but I can know how many people in France will get married within the same period because the individual differences are canceled. Likewise, if the individual is extremely complex and difficult to study, the group to which he belongs cancels individual differences. As a result, I can demonstrate the necessary connection between the world view of the nobility of the robe, which has elaborated the mental structures of Jansenism, and certain works by Racine. I can also give a very detailed explanation of the genesis and meaning of the latter. In this sense, if one does not relate historical facts and major cultural creations (which are also historical facts) to a collective subject, it is impossible for him to comprehend or to study their meaningfulness. If you wish, during the discussion we will pose the problem of average works that are miscellanies inasmuch as they closely reflect the individual alone. This is precisely why they are average and, thus, difficult to study.

What is characteristic of non-genetic structuralism, even in its current advanced efforts to introduce the concept of movement and becoming, is the negation of what it calls the "anthropological" subject. What Foucault calls the "anthropological" subject is, if you will, what Althusser would call simply the subject; but it always amounts to the same thing. In Foucault's latest book (*Les Mots et les Choses*, 1970), in which he offers a number of discontinuities, there is, however, a chapter on transformations. There he admits that these discontinuities are only part of an investigative strategy and that beyond such a level there is a whole series of partial transformations that need to be described. But these latter are seen externally. What he would never admit — and here is the crucial element — is the subject that creates these transformations, makes history and elaborates the history of ideas and thought. This it does in order to exist and to adjust its relations to the surrounding world. The entire book treats the anthropological subject with irony, as if it were manifestly unscientific. Pardon me for pointing out the obvious, but when someone speaks, it is a living, flesh-and-blood human being who does so, an "anthropological" subject. The question to raise is can we study human facts beyond their meaning, that is, beyond their functional relation to these anthropological subjects.

Only here, at the level of the subject, are there a whole series of particularly important problems. The individualist tradition of classical philosophy, whether empiricist or rationalist, was based on the individual subject who stood opposite a given world. This subject did not make the world. He could judge it, but at the most he could only act on it in a technical way. The basic epistemological principle for these philosophies was that value judgments were separate from judgments of fact. Poincaré gave it its classical formulation: "One can never draw an imperative from two indicatives." True. The only question is, are there indicative judgments *in the human sciences*. Obviously, if the subject is individual, the world seems already made, a thing which is different from him. For example, I once could have quoted a Cartesian grammar by Bruneau from which I learned that *je* is a pronoun that does not have a plural form and *nous* always means *je* and *tu*, i.e., a *moi*-subject and a *toi*-object of my thoughts.

Actually, things are quite different. When philosophy began to doubt that the world was made by men, and when the likes of Kant and Husserl began to claim that the world is not simply an object in front of man but that man helps to build it, it became necessary to introduce the basic philosophical category (I would say "scientific monster") of the transcendental subject. The transcendental subject is non-empirical and has created the world, but in such a way that when I (as empirical subject) am faced with the former, I find it already made. It is very easy to criticize the transcendental subject and to show that it does not exist. But what if one replaces this individual subject with a collective one, the *transindividual* subject? Here, for example, we may recall the case of Peter, John and James lifting the stone, the nobility of the robe that elaborated the categories that Racine used in writing his plays and Pascal his *Pensées* and the historical development of the French bourgeoisie which ended in the Revolution of 1789. Then we have empirical subjects which *really* create the world. It is empirical men who have built this house, the roads, society, institutions and mental categories. Now the situation is quite different and we must face the methodological question of knowing what the status of scientific reflection is.

Let us for a moment say that you accept the thesis of the trans-individual subject which, ultimately, is the subject of all historical action. For example, let us accept the fact that Pascal's *Pensées*, Racine's plays and Jansenist thought (from which they derive) are connected to the nobility of the robe. It is then necessary to take into account that the nobility of the robe had more than an external society in mind when envisaging the world and society. It also projected its own situation there. Let us admit that Marx's thought derives from the proletarian thought of his epoch — this should be discussed, I myself am not so sure. The Marxist theory of capitalist society, then, is one in which the proletariat considers its own involvement in its analysis of that society. There is no radical separation of subject and object.

The subject is also part of the object of thought and, conversely, the object (capitalist society) is part of the mental structure of the subject. For the human sciences, then, science is at least partially affected by social consciousness. When dealing with the human sciences, cultural creation and historical action, one cannot separate science from consciousness, theory from practice, and judgments of fact from value judgments. Auguste Comte once criticized the idea of introspection, the idea of the individual subject who studies himself: if I study my anger, the study will turn out bad because my anger will upset it; my anger is false because the investigation interrupts it. Up to a certain point, the same is true for the human sciences. This does not at all mean that we must abandon a rigorous approach, but rather that we must be aware that the radical opposition between subject and object and fact and value is absolutely illusory, not to say more. In one of my books I mentioned the example of Durkheim. Thinking that he could make sociology an objective science, the great sociologist tried to show how in his study on crime. He said, "In my study, I will define crime conventionally as any act penalized by society. Here is a category of facts that I can study sociologically." But it is evident that he had already created a category of facts in which Jesus, Socrates, a revolutionary or any individual whatever who tries to change society and is penalized, belong to the same category. In the same way, one could analyze any work in the human sciences to show that subject and object, value judgments and judgments of fact are closely connected, without thereby denying their relative (but very relative) autonomy. It is also necessary that one be aware of this interaction. In this sense, then, we must study human facts.

The first scientific problem is that of isolating significant objects. If I am a sociologist of literature, it is because my means were scarce and because the great works of literature and philosophy empirically yielded these significant objects. If, however, it is much more difficult to study them in the human sciences, where a thousand or ten thousand people are involved, the methodological principle is the same.

Here I arrive at the second and third alternatives, those of comprehension and explanation, continuity and discontinuity, and diachrony and synchrony. There are others, but most likely I will not have the time to consider them today.

If I propose to study a significant, functional structure, I must isolate the way it is structured. First, I will have to isolate the significant structural model or scheme...at the base of this phenomenon, this social, historical, economic or cultural fact. Then I must explain it by tracing its functionality in a larger reality. I would, above all, insist on the comprehension-explanation coupling. French and especially German academic philosophy have often formulated the following alternative: either we take up the comprehensive and descriptive sciences — like phenomenology and non-genetic structuralism — or we renounce comprehension and take up the traditional method of the natural sciences, thus relying on explanation.

Recently, the critic Pierre Daix said, Goldmann explains and thus he does not try to comprehend. He relates Racine's theater to the nobility of the robe, thus he is not interested in the literary quality of Racine's plays. Obviously, this is as false a division as that of the subject from the object and judgments of fact from judgments of value. When I bring to light the structure of Racine's plays, I comprehend them. This process, however, is not in the least related to the faculty of sympathy as, for example, such scholars as G. Poulet and Bergson intend it. It is an intellectual process which consists in establishing a conceptual instrument for the comprehension of a literary text, in this instance. If I then insert Racine's plays into the context of Jansenism, I am in a position to explain them. In fact, I explain them by comprehending Jansenism. If I situate the structure of the latter within the nobility of the robe in 17th-century France, I can comprehend it, and I explain Jansenism by relating it to French society and the class relationships making up that society.

I can only explain what I comprehend. Conversely, it also proves true for valid research that I cannot comprehend something if I do not also explain it. If you allow me to digress, sociology and...psychoanalysis have a particular situation. There is a very close relationship between the latter science and dialectical sociology. I am not talking about the Marxism of Althusser or Lacan's psychoanalysis here, since both are attempts to structuralize these sciences by eliminating the categories of the subject and development, both fundamental in Marx and Freud. In speaking about Marx, Hegel and Freud, however, we find quite a number of common elements among them. First of all, for all three, every human fact is meaningful. Whether it be a dream, an act of delirium, a cultural work or a historical process, human facts are the result of a subject's meaningful behavior. Secondly, this latter can only be brought to light by integrating such unintelligible facts into a structure wherein they are related to a large number of other elements. Thirdly, this structure can only be comprehended in its development (biographical for Freud, historical for Hegel and Marx). Here, however, differences arise. Freud, who studied the libido..., only recognized the individual subject. However, what creates problems in the Freudian system is this: when he turns to history, culture and religion, he still bases his approach on the individual subject which, aspiring to certain things, also ends up being censured and repressed. Freud has never successfully explained why a being who lives outside of society creates both society and the taboo of incest. But if you begin with the idea that at a given moment of historical development there appeared the division of labor, the symbolic function and the capability of making oneself understood, then even the Freudian schema can explain the origin of the incest taboo. There must be many people if one wants to act corporately, defend oneself, or build shelters. Freud himself has demonstrated this. And I think he is right in saying that the libido tends to fasten the little animal on others who are immediately close by, i.e., to create little groups. The large group is only maintained through the prohibition of immediate relations and through the creation of more distant ones.

Well, then, human behavior is meaningful in two respects: libidinal behavior, which is related to the individual subject, and collective behavior, which is related to transindividual subjects and is responsible for historical action. Of course, the two subjects do conflict. When this occurs, there are two possibilities: the libido and its level of meaning will either overcome and disorganize social consciousness, and then one has the phenomenon of alienation; or rigorously coherent and socially derived structures will be created in which the libido is not a distorting factor, and then one has the phenomenon of genius. Halfway between these two extremes are you and me and all those who are neither madmen nor geniuses, nor creators of important works.

At this point a very precise problem arises. As you know, one of Freud's crucial books is called *Traumen Deutung*, which was first translated into French as the *Science des Rêves*. Modern psychoanalysts have since learned that in the dictionary, *Deutung* is defined as "interprétation." It then became necessary to say, "the interpretation of dreams." Finally, though, the translator was right because there is no distinction between interpretation and explanation in Freud's book. Even after a psychoanalyst has exhaustively interpreted the manifest structure of a dream, it is still without meaning. He must still refer back to the dream's context in order to make sense out of it. Explanation and interpretation remain inseparable to the very end. This is because the libidinal level of consciousness is not autonomous. In man, the libido assimilates consciousness. The latter is not an essential structure for libidinal life. Conversely, when dealing with a major cultural or literary work, it is absolutely essential that one also explain it, i.e., analyze the relation between the nobility of the robe and Pascal and Racine, between the court aristocracy and Molière. Once the investigation is secured, though, the structures of social consciousness tend to become autonomous, so that by the end of my analysis I can explain the meaning of great literary works, like the plays of Racine. But every attempt to relate the meaning, the structure, of a cultural work to the libido seems absolutely ineffective and non-functional, or so approximatively functional that it has little scientific interest. I will tell you why. If, for an instant, I think that psychoanalytic explanation has accounted for the whole of a work, it will never succeed in telling me how this work differs from that of a madman which is based on a similar complex. The latter effort is, by definition, ahistorical and non-aesthetical. What is much more important, though, is that it never succeeds in accounting for the whole work; and the partial success it does have is usually rather generic.... Individual elements do not play a role that goes beyond the historical. What I want to point out here, however, is that the comprehension-explanation duality is a false alternative. A scientific investigation of history must always take place on two levels, that of the object to be comprehended and that of the immediately englobing structure, where meaning is born and proves functional. In other words, both comprehension and explanation are necessary throughout the investigation.

This brings us to the final alternatives with which I will deal today and which are at the center of the current discussion on non-genetic structuralism: diachrony and synchrony, continuity and discontinuity.

As you know, according to non-genetic structuralists, the attempt on the part of 19th-century historians to study phenomena diachronically, on the basis of their development, is a Hegelian illusion. On the contrary, for the former, scientific studies should be synchronic. Structures should be studied apart from their development. But, if all reality is a process and if the scientific study is the study of a process resulting from men's actions, one must discover what changes. One cannot study a process without knowing what object is being investigated. Due to the act of perception, all human activity is obliged to create invariants that are objects. These invariants are created at all levels of thought. If we want to understand history, we must consider it as a structuring process. Once this latter is approached, however, or once reality is modified, we must consider it a structuring process that is no longer rational or functional except insofar as it is oriented toward new structures. Thus, such structural concepts as feudalism, capitalism and the tragic vision are necessary for studying their becoming and the way in which collective subjects have changed them. Certainly, the idea of a purely diachronic study, which forgoes systems and structures, is scientifically impossible and inadequate. Furthermore, since reality is always in the process of being structured and destructured, a purely synchronic study, which deals with structures apart from the subjects that transform them, is equally inadequate. Evidently, an important priority exists that one must admit — it is one of the constant arguments of Althusser's followers — but only provisionally, on the level of research: the investigation of the invariant's structure which then allows one to study its genesis. One should have a more or less advanced concept of the structure (the invariants) in order to be able to study their variations. One of Althusser's arguments is that *Das Kapital* is a study of the structure of capitalist society apart from its development. We are quite aware of this, but Marx died before completing his work. From all that he wrote, we know that it was, for him, the only way to accede to a study of development, to a study of history. All of his writings assert the necessity of a historical — synchronic — study which, nevertheless, only makes sense insofar as it establishes the structures which men transform. History is the object of structuring processes and these cannot be studied if one has not first established models. Inversely, however, structures are only provisional, the result of men's behavior in precise and concrete situations which they themselves transform within given structures. In this way, they create new structures. In other words, there is a discontinuity which explains transformations and continuity. There is a diachronic aspect that alone can explain synchrony and a synchronic aspect that can be understood only in the light of a diachronic process. It is evident, then, that at the most the synchronic aspect is privileged at the outset of one's research. But this is very temporary. To privilege it in a more fundamental way, to reject the diachronic aspect and, above all, an investigation of the subject, to limit the diachronic aspect to a mere description of transformations, is to never understand how the latter were brought about and who is responsible for them. The essential criticism of this type of structuralism was formulated in May 1968 by a student who wrote on the blackboard, "Structures don't take to the streets." He had something very specific and immediate in mind. It is true, though, that at the level of historical action, in the street, there are only those who act, who create structures and transform them (obviously, one's sentiments and thoughts are structured).

In this sense, and I would like to end here, the great difference between current structuralism and genetic structuralism is the negation of functionality and meaning. I do not want to discuss Foucault's latest book, which abandons this direction but still holds to the negation of the subject, the minimum common denominator of all non-genetic structuralism. The work of most non-genetic structuralists is the mere description of means. A given number of means in the various domains exists for the human being, and in a very precise way one studies the possible combination of these means. One would like to study all of them, but they are innumerable. One finally studies a given number of them in each particular area and what basically remains is a duality, an opposition, the difference. In reality, however, human and historical facts are meaningful — perhaps apart from linguistic structures that are universally human because they presume communication but which do not have their own particular meaning. (Language does not love or hate, it is neither pessimistic nor optimistic because its function is to permit love or hate, hope or despair.) The objects that non-genetic structuralists study are chosen in such a way that they are not meaningful. Eventually, when meaning occasionally does appear, it is so secondary and partial that it practically loses all scientific value. At best, that arises from a sort of intuitionism.

For example, one of the objects in literature which structuralists are now engaged in studying is the *récit*. There is a special issue of *Communications* (No. 8, 1968) on the *récit* (the art of fabulation), with a long introduction by Barthes. For him, however, what is the *récit*? It can be an epic, a novel, a short story or a detective story. The *récit*, finally, is what all these genres have in common, i.e., at the strategic level where the object under study is without meaning — because the epic is something other than the novel and the novel something other than a comic strip. Their common denominator is not in the least meaningful. The most it can offer is an analysis of the James Bond texts or detective novels. There is the basic problem.

Another example: by way of criticizing the traditional methods of literary criticism, Foucault raises an obvious problem.

Who is the author? What is the work? How is one to delimit it? Is it everything the writer has published? In this case, *Le Neveu de Rameau* (*Rameau's Nephew*) is not a part of Diderot's work because he did not publish it (this is the author's example). Is it everything the author has written? Then the laundry list found in such important texts as Kant's *Opus postumum* is relevant. How does one know what to study? Hence, the idea that there is no rigorously defined work. The answer, though, is very simple. The work is a significant structure. If, for example, you are seeking the significant structure of Pascal's work, there are at least two: the *Provinciales* and the *Pensées*. As is true of all the human sciences, you isolate the significant structure of the *Provinciales* by discovering the collective subject that makes it functional. In this case, it is the moderate Jansenist group centered around Arnauld and Nicole. In the case of the *Pensées*, it is the extreme group gathered around Barcos and Mother Angélique. The two subjects are different, the common element is Pascal. Likewise, you can eliminate the laundry list, which is not part of Kant's work, because it cannot be integrated into this significant structure. In the same way, you can integrate *Le Neveu de Rameau* into Diderot's work. You see the extent to which all the problems, which at first seemed insoluble, become solvable as soon as you begin with the idea that it is a question of studying structures, significant structures, in relation to a subject.

To conclude, I would like to insist upon another fact. If you return to the combinatory study of means, which makes up the greater part of non-genetic structuralist analyses, you will find yourself somewhat in the situation where, for example, you have a pile of boards, metal tubes and nails without knowing what it is all for. Perhaps it is meant to be a scaffolding, but for what? If you know that a house or a bridge is to be built, then you can easily understand the combination that has been used. If, however, you systematically and methodologically eliminate the question of meaning and genesis, then, of course, you will remain at the very arbitrary level of combinatory descriptions. Perhaps, too, these are the least interesting or the most false or are only true by chance, through a correct intuition. Intuition, though, is not a scientific method.

I would still like to have spoken to you about other false

alternatives (like the one between freedom and determinism, between subjectivity and objectivity, which has dominated the epoch of Sartre), but time is pressing and perhaps we will take them up during the discussion. Throughout this conference I have tried to show you one thing. If we want to work in the field of the positive human sciences, these false alternatives must be avoided. Above all, we must refuse such principles as the elimination of the subject or the object, every attempt, finally, to eliminate one of the basic aspects of reality. We must study reality as a process made by men, created by them, and having a human meaning. It is precisely a question of positive comprehension, i.e., of understanding ourselves.

2. The Epistemology of Sociology

In the human sciences, the moment one approaches any problem at a sufficiently general level, one finds oneself in a cricle where the researcher himself is part of the society that he intends to study and that plays a pre-eminent role in the elaboration of his mental categories. (Jean Piaget has shown the existence of this circle on many levels, notably in the classification of the sciences and their interdependence.)

We encounter this same circle in broaching the study of sociological knowledge and that of the sociology of knowledge. If, like all other scientific disciplines, sociology is a science based on an aggregation of categories forming an intellectual structure, then these categories and this structure are themselves social facts that sociology brings into relief. Inversely, mental categories, which are also social facts, justify sociological thought in their turn.

Yet, if we are in the presence neither of a vicious circle nor an insurmountable obstacle here, we still have a particular situation in the human sciences from which no researcher can escape. This situation implies certain epistemological and methodological consequences concerning the relation between thought and action in the socio-historical realm and, thus, it involves the very structure of sociological objectivity.

Furthermore, when we approach the study of society in general, and the facts of individual and collective consciousness in particular, we must never lose sight of the following points:

1. If the concept of "collective consciousness" is an operation notion indicating an aggregation of individual consciousnesses and their relationships, it does not correspond to any reality that could be situated outside these consciousnesses. As Marx said, "Above all, one must avoid making 'society' an abstraction in relation to individuals. The individual is a social essence. His exteriorization — even if it does not appear in the immediate form of an exteriorization accomplished in common with others — is,

then, an exteriorization and confirmation of social life. The life of the individual man and the life of the species are not different."[1] And Piaget reiterates this: "Sociology must consider society as a whole, although this whole, as distinct from the sum of individuals, may only be the aggregation of the relations or interactions among these individuals."[2]

2. Socio-historical reality is a structured aggregation of the conscious behavior of individuals — whether this consciousness be true or false, adequate or inadequate — within a determinate natural and social environment.

3. The structuring process results from the fact that individuals — and the social groups that they constitute (groups formed by individuals finding themselves related to one another and, in certain more or less important aspects, in similar situations) — seek to give unitary and coherent responses to the aggregation of problems posed by their relations with the surrounding environment. Or to put it another way, they tend by their action (praxis) to establish a balance between themselves and this environment.

The results of the thesis are:

A. Every fact of consciousness is strictly bound in an immediate or relatively mediated way to praxis, just as all praxis is mediately or immediately, explicitly or implicitly, bound to a specific structure of consciousness.

B. Just as the psychologist must conceive of an individual's psychological life as a complex effort tending toward an integral but difficult balance between the subject and his environment, so the sociologist must study every social group in an effort to find an integral and coherent response to the problems common to all members of the group in relation to their social and natural environment.

Obviously, for each individual, these problems are only one part of his consciousness, the whole of which is connected to all the groups to which he belongs. Thus, each individual is a mixture and a source of a different structuring process in relation to other members of the group.

All the same, the sociologist can make an abstraction of these

---

1. See Karl Marx, "Economic and Philosophical Manuscripts," in Marx, *Early Writings* (New York, 1975), p. 350.
2. Jean Piaget, *Psychologie de l'intelligence* (Paris, 1952), p. 186.

differences in order to disengage the reality of a common process, of a relatively thwarted attempt by each individual consciousness to provide a coherent solution to an aggregation of problems common to all members of the group.

C. Within these observations, which are valid for all social groups, certain groups present a privileged character both by their conscious life and by their social and historical praxis. For these groups praxis is oriented toward a global structuring of society, that is, toward a certain balance among the constitutive groups of the entire society, and between the society and the physical world.

The conscious aspect of the life of these groups appears to be the essential factor in the genesis of their cultural life and praxis, a decisive element of historical life.

It appears equally true that, at least with regard to much of modern history, it is social classes that have constituted these privileged groups.

4. The existence of social groups constitutes a process of equilibration between a collective subject and a social and natural environment. Thus, the group is a structure within the wider relative totality that encompasses it, while its own constitutive elements are relative totalities in themselves, albeit more structures.

Subjectivity and Objectivity: The establishing of facts and values

On the basis of the fact that every sociologist himself belongs to a social group, will himself be one of the constitutive elements of a structure that will be another element of study, traditional dialectical thinkers — notably Hegel and Lukacs — speak about the identity of the subject and object in action and historical thought. In this perspective, the study of society would be a positive body of knowledge in which the collective subject could itself be known through an individual mind: it would, therefore, be a type of consciousness.

For reasons to be indicated later, this apparently extreme thesis is opposed to the inverse position — in our view, a completely wrong one — of the possibility of attaining a degree of objectivity in the social sciences similar to that in the natural sciences.

Indeed, all social reality is simultaneously constituted by

material and intellectual facts which, in turn, structure the consciousness of the researcher and naturally imply value judgments. That is why a rigorously objective study of society appears impossible. The formula "the identity of the subject and the object" is too general, given that the value judgments that make up a part of the object studied can be mediately or immediately related with the values that structure the consciousness of the researcher. Thus, for example, even if total objectivity is beyond the reach of contemporary French sociologists, the maximum attainable degree of objectivity varies, depending upon whether one studies the Eskimos, the thought of Marsile Ficin, the Florence of the Medicis, or contemporary transformations of the French proletariat.

That is why it is necessary to isolate as much as possible the specific degree of identity between the subject and object in each instance and thereby isolate the degree of accessible objectivity. Furthermore, this relationship between values and social reality implies a complementary result. If values structure the researcher's consciousness and introduce an element of distortion, the latter's thought in its turn also constitutes an element of reality. By the simple fact of its elaboration and expression, the researcher's thought modifies reality, mostly in an insignificant way, but at times appreciably.

Beginning with the relationship between thought and praxis, then, how can we pose the problem of objectivity with regard to knowledge in general, and the human sciences in particular?

From Marx up to the contemporary works of Jean Piaget, many epistemological and historical investigations have established the strict bond between the categorical structure of human thought and praxis, a relation as valid for daily thought and the natural sciences as for the human sciences. In the case of the natural sciences, nevertheless, we can today speak of objective thought to the extent that its goal, man's mastery over nature and the resulting categorical structure, is the same for all actually existing groups. That is why physics is practiced the same way in Moscow and Washington, Paris and Warsaw. The differences, which are in the final instance secondary, depend upon the scientific and professional education of the researchers, upon their talent, their intelligence and, to a certain extent, upon the social network of university relations, their traditions, and so on. These differences do not, at any rate, depend upon the fundamental structure of global societies and the categories that such a structure engenders.

Without any serious danger of distortion, the physicist concerned with the problems of method can place himself exclusively on the level of theoretical research without concerning himself with the problems of his relationship to praxis, since this relation is implicit in the discussion.

But the situation is very different in the human sciences. Today, man's growing mastery over nature is unanimously accepted by nearly everyone. When one analyzes social life, however, the values determining the categorial structure of consciousness nearly always have a specific and, thus, deforming character. In other words, by making this consciousness abstract, one implicitly forms an ideology rather than a positive science.

Thus, one of the most important tasks of the serious researcher is to know and to make known to others his value judgments by making them explicit. This will help him attain the maximum degree of objectivity that is subjectively accessible to him the moment he writes. This will also help future researchers working in the same perspective and will afford them a better comprehension of reality. They will more easily be able to use his works and go beyond them.

Specific value judgments are inevitably part of all historical and sociological research, either in an explicit or implicit way, and this participation has an immediate and technical character in the development and elaboration of ideas in social life. Thus, even the most honest, scrupulous and critical sociological study can be characterized as an explicit or implicit wager, both theoretically and practically: theoretically with regard to the maximum possible conformity to the object studied; practically, with regard to the possibility of transforming society or stabilizing it.

Structures and world views

Most concrete sociological or psychological studies from Marx and Freud to Piaget are inspired by genetic structuralism. In other words, they are based on the hypotheses stated above: first, to be aware that one's subjective life is closely bound to praxis; second, that this life is presented on both the individual and collective levels under the form of dynamic realities oriented toward a coherent equilibrium between the subject and its surrounding environment, that is, toward structuring processes; third, that within these global processes one's subjective life, and within this the realm of thought, constitutes a relative totality in its turn, a structuring process directed toward a significant and coherent state of equilibrium.

In the privileged case of groups oriented toward a global organization of society, we have called these psychic structurations world views.

By limiting ourselves to the structuring processes of world views and to their conceptual expression — theory and value scales (there are also imaginary expressions such as literature and art) — it seems evident that the latter are not sums of independent elements, isolated atoms coupled to each other. On the contrary, they are aggregations, the constitutive parts of which are inter-dependent and bound together by specific rules and have limited possibilities of transformation.

World views could not be purely individual facts. No matter how great the creative imagination of an individual may be, given the limits of his life and his experiences, he could at best only partially elaborate such an aggregation of categories. This process of elaboration is a slow and complex one, usually spread out over several generations. It presupposes the joint praxis of a considerable number of individuals who constitute a social group and, when we are dealing with the elaboration of a world view, a privileged social group.

Such a world view constitutes the "collective consciousness" of a group and this general formula must, in each particular case, be replaced by the "consciousness of a specific group." Still, it is obvious that a world view exists only in the individual consciousness of those making up the group. In each individual this world vision is presented under the form of a relatively global apprehension of the group, as the process of the aggregate's structuration. It follows that a sociology of knowledge must, above all, study the socio-historical processes of the structuring process of large systems at the general level characteristic of the systems of formal logic and at the level of more specific and particular totalities, world views. It follows also that this could only be done by reconnecting these processes of intellectual genesis to the universal praxis of individuals as such (for formal logic) and to the specific social praxis of certain privileged groups, notably, social class (for world views).

Self-regulation and progress — accommodation and assimilation

Furthermore, one must always remember that when dealing with social facts in general and with the processes of intellectual structuration, which, within the tendencies of global balance, constitutes the genesis of world views, in particular, one is dealing with processes of an average duration governed by a rather complex dynamism. This has been identified in history by Marx and in psychology by Piaget.

As a world vision is being elaborated, and this process is part of a larger one in which a collective subject attempts to achieve a balance with its social and natural environment, opposite but complementary processes will sooner or later be manifested. Marx has called this tension the conflict between the relations of production and the development of productive forces. On the psychological level, Piaget has called it the antagonism between assimilation into the existing mental structures and accommodation to the structures of the external world.

In fact, every process of structuration implies the tendency to incorporate into the state of equilibrium a greater and greater area of the surrounding social and physical world. This tendency, however, can conflict with three kinds of obstacles, two of which are originally exogenous and one endogenous:

I. The fact that certain sectors of the external world do not lend themselves to integration into the structure being elaborated.

II. The fact that certain structures of the external world are transformed in such a way that, although they may have been able to be integrated before, this integration becomes increasingly difficult and finally impossible.

III. The fact that individuals in the group, who are responsible for generating the processes of equilibrium, transform the surrounding social and physical environment, thereby creating situations that hinder the continuation of the structuring processes generating them.

For these three reasons, every process of equilibrium sooner or later ceases to constitute the optimal response to the need to find a significant balance between the collective subject and its environment. Phenomena will then appear with the process that Piaget calls accommodation to reality. This is a structuring process oriented toward a new equilibrium, one better adapted than the previous one to the present praxis of the group.

In this sense, particularly with regard to the sociology of knowledge and the life of the spirit, the sociologist nearly always finds himself faced with extremely complex processes. More precisely, he is faced with the deviation of old structuring processes and the old equilibrium, as well as with the gradual birth of the structuring process of a new equilibrium.

From the perspective of concrete research, this situation poses the problem of knowing to what extent empirical facts can be described on the basis of the old and deviated structuring process (which Piaget would call accommodation) and to what extent they can be described on the basis of the new structuring process still charged with the surviving elements of the old process, which it has replaced.

In philosophical language, this is the problem designated by Hegel and Marx as the passage from quantity to quality.

Isolating the Object of Study

In his practical research, the sociologist is immediately confronted by a very difficult problem: that of isolating synchronically and diachronically the object of his study.

As we have already said, all human reality tends toward an equilibrium that transforms the surrounding world, and the very processes of equilibrium are also transformed by a self-regulatory process making up the new equilibrium. In a less abstract way, one could say that history is made by the effort of human groups to find a coherent and significant aggregate of responses to the problems posed by their relations with the surrounding world. These responses, however, are each time exceeded by the transformations of this surrounding world, which the very praxis of the group carries out and which, by an extension of the range of this praxis, generates new processes of equilibrium. The individuals of the group and their environment, the two elements making up such an orientation toward a meaningful equilibrium, however, are far from being immediate givens for the researcher.

We have here the well-known dialectical distinction between appearance and essence, between the empirical given presented in an abstract way and its concretization through the mediation of the concept.

The data of immediate experience is most often presented to the researcher torn from its global context and, as such, separated from its meaning, that is, its essence. Data can only be made concrete by inserting it into the destructuring process of an old structure and into the structuring process of a new equilibrium. In this way one may judge the objective meaning of data as well as its relative importance in the aggregate.

The first step of such an analysis, then, is to isolate the object to be studied. In other words, one must bring to light a totality in which the objective meaning of a major part of the empirical data under study can be attained. Such a totality will also permit one to study the transformations of this data. We assume, however, that the aggregate of these empirical facts is taken as the starting point of research and that the possibility of accounting for them is the sole objective criterion for judging its validity. It should also be stressed that this initial isolation of the object determines the rest of the analysis and that, frequently, the ideological factor intervenes precisely at this point by influencing the later results of research in advance.

Here is an example: it was impossible to isolate the tragic vision of Pascal's *Pensées* insofar as one was seeking, as most scholars of Pascal were, a valid internal coherence both for *Les Provinciales* and the *Pensées*. It is impossible to understand the specific traits of the First Empire, Stalinism or Nazism on the basis of the idea that there exists a social fact having fixed qualities which, as such, can be studied sociologically under the concept of "dictatorship."

Although the process of isolating the object is unique for each study, there are some general rules. Notably, the objects studied must be significant structures. It is on the basis of their position in the aggregate that specific elements and their transformations may be understood. Then, one must eliminate such typical concepts as "dictatorship," "hierarchy," and "scandal" as well as purely individual facts. The former must be eliminated because they derive from an abstraction based on some common characteristics that have different and even opposite meanings in each particular case; the latter because they remain insufficiently defined so long as they have not been inserted into a wider dynamic totality in which they can be made concrete. Such a totality can eventually be reconciled with other related structures. As a result, between the poles of positivist and abstract sociology and anecdotal history, there is a place for a concrete science of social facts that could only be a historical sociology or a sociological history.

Real consciousness and possible consciousness

Having isolated the object of his research, the scholar finds himself faced with another important problem. In fact, social reality is far too rich and complex to be analyzed in its totality, even in the framework of a validly isolated object. Furthermore, no definitions of the object under study are ever valid in the absolute sense. One always begins with an approximation and, as research continues, one is obliged to modify it. As the structure under study is drawn with more detail, certain facts prove irrelevant while others, which at first seemed out of place, now fit. Thus, the researcher must base himself on two conceptual instruments that only rarely correspond to empirical reality in a sufficiently close way: the balanced and coherent structure toward which the old structuring process was tending, but which is now being superseded, and the structure toward which the principal structuring process is now tending.

In sociology, schematizations such as "feudal society," "capitalist society," "totemism," "Protestantism," and "Jansenism" are at the root of all important research. Obviously, it is clear that there are good and bad schematizations determining the value of practical research. For example, a number of contemporary ethnologists have questioned the validity of the concept "totemism." To prove their position, they will have to replace it with another concept better suited to empirical reality, but this one will also be a schematization.

When studying mental categories and consciousness in general, the most functional schematizations appear to be those corresponding to the concept first elaborated by Marx and Lukacs as *zugerechnetes Bewusstsein* (consciousness as "calculated" or "constructed" by the researcher), a term that we have translated as possible consciousness.

We may, then, conceive of social life as a totality of the processes through which groups of individuals try to achieve a satisfying and coherent equilibrium with their social and natural environment. The facts of consciousness constitute an essential and interdependent part of this effort. These processes, along with their conscious element, come into conflict with innumerable incidental or structural obstacles that make up the empirical environment. Furthermore, these obstacles do not remain purely external but have a distorting effect on the consciousness of the subject.

In the resulting relationship between the subject and his environment, the subject (both on the individual and transindividual levels) never reacts univocally but projects a relatively large gamut of possible responses. Within this gamut different responses can be alternated at will.

Depending on the level of research, the important thing is not to know the effective consciousness of the group at a given moment, but rather the field within which this knowledge and these responses can vary without there being an essential modification of existing structures and processes. If sociological research is not yet able to make an inventory of these possible responses, it can, on the other hand, establish at least two privileged modalities within this field. They are effective consciousness and the maximum possible consciousness (i.e., the maximum degree of knowledge able to admit the processes and structures being studied and still conform to reality, this "maximum" being a crucial conceptual instrument for the understanding of reality).

To carry out this sort of analysis, it is particularly important to study groups oriented toward a global structuration of society. If the secondary processes and structures (i.e., those not absolutely indispensable to the existence of such a group) are neglected at the outset, the maximum possible consciousness compatible with the existence of these basic groups, known historically as social classes, can be determined. It is, moreover, at the level of the possible consciousness of the great classes of modern European society (the proletariat, the bourgeoisie, and even the court aristocracy and the nobility) that this concept has been elaborated and defined, a conceptual instrument that appears to be of primary importance in the understanding of human reality. It is also crucial with respect to the structured grouping of the facts of consciousness, a fact which is particularly obvious when one is dealing with the sociology of cultural creations (literary, artistic and philosophical) and the sociology of political action.

Indeed, if the real consciousness of groups rarely matches their possible consciousness, the great cultural works seem precisely to express this maximum to an advanced and nearly coherent degree (and this on such levels as the concept, the verbal imagination, the visual, etc.). It is this aspect that makes them characteristic of human societies. Thus, cultural works are both collective and individual to the extent that the world view they correspond to has been elaborated over several years and several generations by the collectivity. The author, however, is the first, or at least one of the first, to express this world view at a level of advanced coherence, whether on the theoretical level or on the artistic, by creating an imaginary universe of characters, objects and relations.

This manner of considering the facts of consciousness represents a considerable upheaval in the sociology of culture. Until Lukacs and those inspired by him, in fact, this discipline was oriented toward the research of analogies between the content of the collective consciousness and that of cultural creations. The results were easily foreseeable: similarities were often discovered, but these did not concern the totality of the work and its unity, i.e., its specifically cultural character. Instead, they concerned a relatively large number of partial elements all the more numerous as the work was less original and merely reproduced the author's personal experience without distilling it. But genetic structuralism seeks instead a homology, an intelligible relationship, between the structures of the collective consciousness and the structures of cultural works that express an integral and coherent universe, it being understood that the two rigorously homologous structures can have entirely different contents.

In this perspective it is precisely those works in which the author has completely distilled the experience of the group that prove to approach most closely the structure of a collective consciousness. For this reason also, they are the most accessible to sociological research. But works that reflect only an individual experience usually represent a mixture best studied by a biographical methodology, since they lack a coherent structure. (Far from reflecting the consciousness of his group, the true creator reveals what those in the group were thinking and feeling unbeknownst to themselves, i.e., where they were implicitly and confusedly headed. For example, in order to know whether or not the works of Pascal or Racine are Jansenist, it is not necessary to compare them to the thought of Arnauld or Nicole, but to the possible consciousness of the group to which they belong. This would permit one to show that the their works go beyond the thought of other Jansenists, and it is in relation to them that one measures the degree of Jansenism in the other characters studied by anecdotal history.)

Similarly, the concept of possible consciousness is of primary importance for sociology and, particularly, for political action. The latter, in fact, is a conscious attempt to intervene in social life in order to transform it. It is true that in a stable period a politician wishing to be elected or to stay in office can limit himself to an intuitive or scientific knowledge of the real consciousness of groups. Every attempt to transform the structure of this consciousness, however, poses the problem of its solidarity and the limits in which it can be modified without radically transforming the present structure of these groups. A well-known example illustrates this problem. Up to 1917, international socialist thought was rather strictly oriented toward the maintenance and development of a state-controlled or cooperative agricultural system. But in 1917 the success of the Russian Revolution depended essentially on the possibility of the Bolsheviks obtaining the peasants' support. That is why Lenin radically modified these traditional positions by explaining to his comrades that the idea of the great exploitation of the land went so far beyond the possible consciousness of the Russian peasant that the revolution proved impossible. Nor could they accept it in the future. In other respects, however, such as their loyalty to the czar, their spirit of obedience, etc., their consciousness could be changed rather easily. Analyses of the same kind could undoubtedly be elaborated for a number of contemporary political events. They show that positivist sociology, oriented only toward the exploitation of real consciousness, is insufficient and misses the most important aspects of reality.

Comprehension and Explanation

With regard to social facts, the genetic structuralist perspective also clarifies one of the most controversial points concerning methodology in the human sciences. The description of the states of equilibrium toward which particular social processes tend and the attempt to explain why these specific structures have an optimal functional value within a structure of the whole constitutes a positive and rigorous definition of what has often been designated in a vague way by the concept of comprehension.

Frequently, in fact, the latter has been defined only by an affective label, such as sympathy or empathy. Indeed, without denying the variable importance that these factors can have on the researcher and the progress of his work, there are still external and intellectual conditions rigorously defined as the description of the essential relationships between the elements of a structure and the discovery of its optimal functioning.

In this perspective, explanation is no longer a process apart from comprehension. In fact, a structure's optimal function, indispensable to comprehension, is an element of explanation. This function is especially evident when we place ourselves in a genetic perspective rather than a static one. In effect, changes within a structure naturally involve modifications of this optimal function and, implicitly, the major or minor characteristics of the collective subject and its structural characteristics. These changes in the object, i.e., in the environment, can be either of an exogenous or an endogenous origin, as we have already said. In either case, though, these changes entail a new orientation of the structuring process, which in turn requires a new comprehensive description. This means that the comprehensive description of the genesis of a global structure has an explanatory function with regard to the evolution and transformations of the particular structures that make up the global one. According to this perspective, then, comprehension and explanation are one and the same intellectual process, though related to two different points of reference: one an englobing structure and the other an englobed one.

To give an example: the description of the tragic vision and its expression in Pascal's *Pensées* and Racine's tragedies constitutes a comprehensive study of these writings. But the structural and comprehensive description of the Jansenist movement has an explanatory value for the genesis of Pascal's and Racine's writings. Of course, in cases where the dynamism of the transformations is predominantly endogenous, the simple fact of a genetic study at the level of the given structure already has, as such, an explanatory character. More often, however, the origins of the transformation are both exogenous and endogenous. Thus, all serious investigation must explore both the great transformations of the englobing structure and, at as precise a level as possible, the genesis and transformation of the structure constituting the object proper to the work. This is the middle level of research, then, that at which one wishes to disengage only those transformations that have an explanatory value for the englobed structure and not the totality of the englobing structure.

The starting points of research: progress from the abstract to the concrete

Our perspective, then, supports the idea that individual empirical facts must be inserted into a structuring process in order to obtain their meaning and have knowledge of their nature. This process, in turn, can only be known by studying the elements and relationships composing it. By proceeding from the immediate and abstract empirical given — or from the abstract global hypothesis — to concrete and mediated reality, one cannot hope to follow a linear progress which begins from a necessary starting point, whether empirical or rational.

Similarly, to the extent that the facts one proposes to study constitute a structure and not a class, one cannot see rigorously valid definitions for all these facts and for them only.

Class is defined by the closest genus and the characteristics of the species; structure, on the other hand, is defined by the internal description of its states of equilibrium and the genetic analysis of its functionality. In his attempt to define intelligence, Piaget comes up against the same difficulties and concludes: "It remains possible to define intelligence by the direction which its development is oriented to without insisting on the question of limits, which become a matter of stages or of successive forms of equilibrium. Thus, one can simultaneously see it from the viewpoints of the functional situation and the structural mechanism."[3]

In order to reach this point, research must start from several different points of the structuring process as well as from the wider structuring process that surrounds the object to be studied. Further, one must admit that certain starting points are relatively favorable to its progress. One can only advance by successive approximations obtained by a permanent *va-et-vient* between the whole and its parts. Progress in understanding a global structure most often involves the possibility of better understanding its elements. Inversely, progress in understanding the latter permits one to return to the whole in a functional manner.

Since the meaning of every group of facts depends upon their insertion into a structured whole, and since each global structure is, in turn, part of another structure that englobes it, it follows that no genetic structuralist analysis could end up with an exhaustive meaning and explanation. This is also a practical problem that must be resolved in each particular case, that of knowing into what processes of structuration one must insert the facts studied, in view of obtaining a sufficient number of meanings and pertinent explanations to attain the degree of precision proposed.

Determinism and equilibrium

Lastly, we should like to close this enumeration of the basic principles of a dialectical sociology (or, if you will, a structuralist and genetic sociology) by recalling another aspect of the circle with which we began this study.

The sociologist is part of the society he studies and which structures his consciousness. Because of this, it is impossible to separate radically judgments of fact from value judgments in the

---

3. *Psychologie de l'intelligence*, p. 16.

human sciences. It is equally important in doing concrete research to keep in mind the circle constituted by the action of the social conditions on thought and on the praxis of men and the action of praxis on these conditions.

One can always explain the thought or behavior of a group of men by the social conditions of the epoch (although only to a certain extent, not completely, because every aggregate of conditions limits the field of possible responses, but does not engender one univocally determined response). It is just as important, however, that the researcher keep in mind the fact that social life represents an aggregate of processes. To a large extent, social conditions themselves are the result of the praxis of individuals belonging to specific groups. Present praxis, then, modifies the environment. It creates the conditions in which the individuals of various groups will have to act and gives rise to the problems which they will have to resolve in the near future.

Here lies the most important difference between a dialectical sociology and an entirely positivist or mechanist one. Marx, who accounted for it perfectly, formulated it in the third Thesis on Feuerbach: "The materialist doctrine which says that men are the products of circumstances and education, that consequently, transformed men may be the products of other circumstances and of a modified education, forgets that it is precisely men who transform circumstances and that the educator himself needs to be educated."[4]

No determinist, mechanist or simply positivist conception of social life will effectively succeed in explaining why the relative equilibrium once established between the subject and the object does not remain definitive after a period of time elapses.

This type of sociology is obliged to introduce a group of exceptional beings into its scheme (gods, wise men, legislators, social technocrats), to admit the existence of irrational factors beyond the reach of science (accidents, happenings), or to ignore the problem altogether.

A genetic and dialectical perspective, on the other hand, sees here not only one of the essential aspects of the circle within which all reflection on social and historical life finds itself

---

4. Cf. Karl Marx, "Theses on Feuerbach," in Lewis S. Feuer, ed., *Marx and Engels: Basic Writings on Politics and Philosophy* (New York, 1959), p. 244.

necessarily engaged, but also one of the elements that must be positively integrated into research if one wishes to keep in touch with reality. It is on this basis that one can understand why dialectical scholars refuse a narrow and mechanist determination. As Piaget writes, science based on the reflex theory too often tends to forget that from time to time it must really give meat to Pavlov's dog. "Although too often forgotten on the theoretical level, one knows in practice that a conditioned reflex stabilizes itself only to the extent that it is confirmed or sanctioned: a signal associated with food does not give place to a lasting reaction if real food is not periodically given. Thus, the association must be inserted within a total behavior based on needs and their satisfaction (whether real, anticipated, or merely pertaining to a game)."[5]

Dialectical scholars also refuse value judgments and categorical or hypothetical imperatives that are not based on reality. In order to understand social life and to have an effect on it, one must realize that in the social sciences the establishing of facts is bound closely to value judgments, and vice versa. Although we cannot deal with it here, another crucial problem concerns the important and even radical modifications that have brought about two particular structures in our general scheme: liberal capitalist society and advanced capitalist society, both having sectors that function in a nearly mechanical way. The problem involved here is that of reification, a process studied by Marx, Lukacs and myself.

Without pretending to analyze the numerous conceptions of social life that are found in contemporary sociology, we will say only a few words about two of them that appear particularly important and apt in clarifying what we are defending.

If we leave aside the positivist, rationalist and relativist positions (the criticism of which is implicit in the preceding pages), we encounter in contemporary French social thought two positions that enjoy a great notoriety and which are meant to be structuralist or, at least, similar to Marxist though.

First of all, there is the non-genetic structuralism of Lévi-Strauss, particularly as it is developed in *Le Totemisme*

---

5. *Psychologie de l'intelligence*, p. 110.

aujourd'hui and *La Pensée sauvage*. Lévi-Strauss has emphatically insisted upon the structural character of human thought. Still, he has given these structures a purely intellectual character by almost eliminating the problem of their functional relation to praxis.

When dealing with the savage mind or the creation of events in relation to scientific thought, Lévi-Strauss is not concerned with the processes of assimilation or detotalization. The processes of accommodation, the passage from one structure to another having a different content, are completely missing. He relegates the content of structures to the second level and is only interested in their formal and logical aspects — classification, serialization, oppositions, and so forth. In *The Savage Mind* it is often a question of knowing in detail the practices of the societies being studied, but this is only because this knowledge appears to him indispensable for knowing the logical function of the elements within the formal structure of a myth or a world view.

On the other hand, the functional relation between the content or vision of the myth and praxis is not in the least taken into consideration. The result is striking: not only does every genetic and dynamic element disappear from the analysis, but what goes also is every concrete relation between the content and the logical form, between the representations and the real life of individuals. By choosing a strictly objective viewpoint, this type of sociology has simply lost contact with a great part of reality.

Jean-Paul Sartre's position is also close to Marxism. In his *Questions de methode*, he insists at length on the need to insert sociological and anthropological analyses into the concrete reality of human projects, i.e., in the last instance, into praxis. But apart from an entire series of analyses that appear to be contestable, he defines the project, praxis, as a "non-savoir" which, for him, must constitute the basis of every theoretical analysis. In doing so, he appears to remain a prisoner of the rationalist prejudice. According to such a perspective, thought can only seize the static, the fact or the aggregate of facts. It can only deal with structures or processes if it cuts them into pieces and, then, it must look at those from the outside.

Now, it is exactly on this point that the basic opposition between rationalism and dialectical thought is found. Even if they have not exactly adopted Sartre's position, most positivist and rationalist thinkers have always been aware of the fact that their conceptual instruments cannot seize social reality in all its concrete richness and dynamism. Without too much difficulty, they have accepted the irrational element in their theoretical analyses: individual events or diachronic succession, affective states, sympathy, etc. Sartre's "non-savoir" is only one of the most recent of these.

On the other hand, dialectical thought, which is a generalized genetic structuralism, asserts the possibility of conceptualizing and integrating genesis into scientific knowledge. This it does by studying the structuring processes rather than isolated facts or structures. One should look at such structuring processes from the perspective of an individual who is part of them and who becomes more and more aware of his own nature, his place in these processes and the nature of the processes themselves. This he can do in a scientific and positive way rather than from a purely theoretical level aiming at total objectivity, a level at which he remains outside the structuring processes.

By using this method, the researcher undoubtedly knows that he is always within a circle. He knows that he has no absolute and necessary point of departure, that he must always oscillate between the parts and the whole, and that he must always keep in mind the impossibility of radically separating observations from value judgments. This perspective, however, appears to be the only one that allows us to approach what is essential in human reality in a positive, functional and concrete way.

3. The Concept of the Significant Structure in the History of Culture

In the study of human facts, and more particularly philosophical, literary or artistic works (later we will give them the global term "culture"), one finds an internal finality that distinguishes them from the physico-chemical sciences in an essential way. If one examines human facts closely, one must define them according to the general concept of "structure," and add the qualifying term "significant."

In fact, valid works in the areas we have listed above are characterized by an *internal coherence,* an aggregate of necessary relations between the different elements constituting them, and, for the principal works, between content and form. As a result, one cannot study certain elements of such works outside the aggregate of which they are a part and which alone determines their objective nature and meaning. The possibility of accounting for the *necessity* of each element in relation to the significant global structure also constitutes the surest guide for the researcher.[1]

We have said elsewhere:

(a) that this internal structure of great philosophical, literary and artistic works is due to the fact that they express, at a very advanced level of coherence, the global attitudes of man faced with the basic problems posed by interhuman relations and the relations between man and nature. These global attitudes ("world views") are limited in number, although it may be impossible to list or categorize them before a sufficient number of monographical studies is completed;

---

1. "First, there is a *structure* (in the most general sense) when the elements are united in a totality that has specific properties as a totality, and when the properties of the elements depend, entirely or partially, on these characteristics of the totality." Jean Piaget, *Etudes d'epistemologie genetique*, Vol. II, *Logique et equilibre*, p. 34. Piaget believes that "structures" can be interpreted as the product or the result of an autonomous process of equilibration. Basically, we are in complete agreement with him. However, it seems that this limits the meaning of the word "structure" to its static aspect, while the "autonomous processes of equilibration" are themselves only *dynamic* structures whose specific nature the researcher must isolate in each investigation.

(b) that the realization of this or that world view in given epochs results from the concrete situation in which the different human groups through the course of history are found;

(c) that structural coherence is not a static reality but a dynamic virtuality within groups, a significant structure toward which the thought, feelings, and behavior of individuals are directed. This is a structure seldom realized by most groups, but which particular individuals can attain in limited areas when they coincide with the tendencies of the group and push these latter toward their ultimate coherence. (This is the case with certain political or religious leaders, great writers, artists and philosophers.)

Thus, the interdependence of the constituent elements of a work occurs in its own area but within one and the same world view where the problems posed by interhuman relations and the relations between men and nature find a response.[2]

That said, we should like to consider one of the principal methodological problems posed by investigations into this area.

In the history of culture, the problem of structure is, in fact, posed on several levels, the two most important of which we shall consider here.

It is evident that a serious study of great works must primarily strive to bring to light their internal coherence, i.e., their proper structure.

Nor is this anything new, because, implicitly or explicitly, this principle has guided many historians. Already in the 17th century Pascal knew that: "One can build a good physiognomy only by reconciling all our contrasts, and it is not enough to follow a sequence of harmonious qualities without reconciling the opposites. In order to understand the author's meaning, one must harmonize all the contrasting passages. Thus, to understand scripture, one must arrive at a meaning in which all the contrary passages are reconciled. It is not enough to possess one which suits a few harmonious passages, but one which reconciles even the contrasting ones. Every author has a meaning with which all the

---

2. Clearly, these general observations only acquire value through many concrete examples that allow one to draw up a scheme. Of course, the best thing here would be to give some examples. But given the limits of this study, this is unfortunately impossible. We must refer the reader to our works on Kant, Pascal, Racine and Goethe.

contrary passages harmonize, or he has no meaning at all."[3]

Therefore, we are not going to insist too much on a working method already well known and used. At the very most, we shall mention that in the history of philosophy, literature and art the concept of the significant and coherent structure has both a theoretical and normative function. This is so to the extent that it is the principal instrument for comprehending the nature and meaning of works as well as the very criterion that permits us to judge their philosophical, literary or aesthetical value.

In fact, to the extent that a work expresses a coherent world view on the level of the concept or the verbal or sensible image, the work is philosophically, literarily or aesthetically valid.[4] To the extent that one succeeds in isolating the view it expresses, to that extent one can comprehend and interpret it objectively. (That is why, moreover, the scientific interpretation of a work is inseparable from the bringing to light of its philosophical or aesthetic value — or non-value.)

Still, the fact remains that both the theoretical and normative character of the concept of the significant structure in the history of culture poses a problem. In elucidating it, we are led to another, less known and more unusual level of the use of this concept.

In fact, the *theoretical* role of the concept of structure in the human sciences, in keeping with its specificity proper to each area of research, does not represent anything *qualitatively* different in relation to the sciences of nature. Its *normative* function, on the other hand, can be explained only by means of the existence of a finality common to the object and the subject of the study, which are both sectors of human and social reality.

In the natural sciences, the scientist undoubtedly seeks a maximum of intelligibility: nevertheless, it will not occur to him to make that into a norm applicable to the object of his study. Rightly he presumes from the start the existence of a minimum

---

3. Fragment 684.
4. Of course, this does not mean that the latter constitutes the *only* criterion according to which one must judge it. In fact, the criterion of *truth* in philosophy and the corresponding criterion of *realism* in art still exist. It is not any less true that while a scientific theory loses all value once it is regarded as false, a conceptual system can be erroneous without thereby losing its philosophical value, just as a poetic work or a work of art can be completely foreign to all realism (yet, this latter is only realized in modern society for certain romantic works) without thereby losing any of its aesthetic value.

degree of intelligibility without which science, as well as life, would be impossible. Further, in his research he gambles on the fact that the intelligibility of the natural world far surpasses this minimum and approaches total intelligibility. Yet, his task consists mainly in adapting his theories to reality. One does not find the astronomer asserting, on the normative level, that the planets should have a circular trajectory, or that they should all have the same number of satellites.

Inversely, when one is dealing with the human sciences — notably, the history of culture — the principal concept of intelligibility (that of *significant structure*) represents both a reality and a norm. This is so precisely because it simultaneously defines the actual dynamic and the end toward which this totality (human society) tends, a totality that includes both the work to be examined and the researcher who studies it.

One cannot assume that nature evolves progressively toward legal, geometric or causal structures. Whereas the hypothesis of a history dominated by tendencies toward more and more extensive, coherent and significant structures up to the final transparent society, uniquely composed of similar structures, is one of the principal *positive* hypotheses in the study of human realities.

This explains why the historian of works constituting culture, or more exactly cultures, could be content only to use the concept of the significant structure at the level of immanent interpretation. This is because a similar immanent interpretation can, in any event, give satisfying results only for philosophical, literary or artistic masterpieces — i.e., for those creations which, in their own area, have achieved an *almost rigorously coherent structure*. This the historian could strictly isolate, with exceptional luck, if he were to study the work alone. Next, because even in such an instance the work is part of an aggregate of greater significant structures, the illumination of which enormously facilitates the work of the researcher.

In *theory*, one cannot deny the possibility of isolating the internal structure of Pascal's *Pensées*, for example, or the theater of Racine, through the exclusive study of the texts, a study which would end up with an adequate comprehension of their meaning. In *reality*, however, such a success could be the result only of exceptional intelligence or luck, and a scientific methodology could in no way limit itself to this.

It would, perhaps, be best to illustrate this with a concrete example. By appealing to our own experience, it seems evident that we could never have arrived at the results we ended up with in our study of the texts of Pascal and Racine if we were not helped by the research of greater significant structures, i.e., the different Jansenist currents of opinion, Jansenism as a whole, social classes in the reigns of Louis XII and Louis XIV, and their struggles at the economic, social and political levels.

Pascal's *Pensées* and Racine's *Brittanicus, Bérénice, Phèdre* and *Athalie* are undoubtedly most rigorously structured and coherent works. Still, it would be difficult to say as much for the other Racinian plays or *all* of the fragments of the *Pensées* taken by themselves. On the other hand, *Les Provinciales* expresses a world view different from that of the *Pensées*.

At the start of his research, the historian who finds himself before this collection of texts is immediately confronted by two principal difficulties:

(a) How to distinguish what is essential in each of these writings — what is part of the coherent structure — from what is secondary; what is found in the work for one of several reasons other than that of internal necessity.

(b) Even assuming — without conceding it — that an immanent study of the text might succeed in separating the essential from the secondary elements by intuitive methods, the no less difficult problem remains of the limitation within which these essential elements of those which pertain to the same significant structure or to related ones, and elements also essential but pertaining to structures more or less different from the first. Thus, *Bérénice* and *Britannicus* are two complementary expressions of one and the same tragic world view, but *Phèdre* expresses another type of tragic view which is related to the *Pensées*. As for *Athalie* or the *Provinciales*, they express a dramatic view, related to the tragic by its place within this

---

5. It is obvious that once the structure of the work is isolated, this separation is very easy to make. But it is precisely a matter of the start of the research and of the possibilities of isolating the structure at a moment when nothing yet permits one to say that such a passage is more important than another for the comprehension of the work.

significant global structure, which one could call the Jansenist ideology.

From the practical viewpoint, it is immediately apparent that superhuman intelligence and intuition are necessary to isolate this entire aggregate of structural relations (the expression of which is essential for understanding the works in question) simply by means of textual studies, no matter how profound and prolonged they may be.

But, as soon as one is no longer content to study just the texts, the problem becomes, if not simplified entirely, at least no more difficult than the problem researchers encounter daily in any area of scientific research. It becomes possible to apply the same research principle of significant global structures to the larger totalities of which the texts are only an element. In the case mentioned, we very quickly came up with the first decisive result when, trying to insert the writings of Racine and Pascal into the aggregate of the Jansenist movement and its thought, which was nothing new (most historians having already attempted to do so before us), we inquired as to the significant structure — the essence — of what was customarily called Jansenism (without very well knowing what it consisted of).

Naturally, there is no need to make a detailed history of our research here. Suffice it to say that we were quickly able to isolate one of Jansenism's central themes, "the rejection of society and the world." The dynamic reality of this theme ended with the internal structuring of this movement into four currents: moderate, centrist, and two differently formed extremist currents of which, for a long time, historians had seen only one — the centrist — and only recently (thanks to the work of M. Orcibal) a second — the moderate current.

Now, among the works that interest us, only *Les Provinciales, Esther,* and to a certain extent *Athalie* are connected to the centrist current, and none is related to the moderate one. This explains the difficulties encountered by most historians of philosophy, religion and literature in accounting for the Jansenism of the *Pensees* and the theater of Racine.

It is at this point that the history of our work appears methodologically interesting. In the theater of Racine and in Pascal's *Pensées*, one finds attitudes toward social life and the state and toward problems (the logic of contradiction and the moral conflict of duties) that are entirely different from those attitudes encountered in the known and explored sectors of Jansenism. This led us to formulate the hypothesis of the existence of at least another current within this movement that was hitherto unknown to historians. With the discovery of the texts of Barcos, an entire series of the most controversial historical events of Jansenism and the life of Pascal have been clarified. These texts allowed us to see, almost at once, the internal structure of the literary and philosophical works we wished to study.

We shall cite a single concrete illustration: for three centuries, historians have debated the problem of Pascal's attitude toward the church during the last months of his life and the possibility of reconciling the two apparently contradictory testimonies of the *Ecrit*. This expressed a total refusal to sign the Formulary and his avowal to Beurier (to whom Pascal had asserted his own submission two years earlier) that he accepted all the decisions of the church (which had demanded that he sign the Formulary).

The discovery of the fact that Barcos and his partisans defended a *rigorously coherent* position, which implied both the decision to sign the Formulary and the refusal to do so, permitted us not only to clarify the problem of Pascal's last years but also to bring to light the internal structure of Racinian theater and the *Pensées*.

One need think only of the similar situation of Andromache committing herself to Hector and to the saving of Astyanax, or of Titus, who had to remain emperor and yet not separate himself from Bérénice. Each of these requirements seems contradictory.

When isolating the coherence and the internal structure of literary, artistic and philosophical works attached to the history of ideological, social, political and economic movements, one can see the major importance of investigating significant structures on the level of these movements.

Fundamentally, one is dealing here with the concrete application of two general principles. These, it seems, must guide any serious study in the area of the historical and social sciences, namely:

(a) Every human fact is inserted into a certain number of

significant global structures. The discovery of these alone permits one to know its objective nature and meaning.

(b) To delimit an aggregate of facts which make up such a significant structure in reality, and to separate the essential from the accidental in the raw empirical given, it is essential to insert these still poorly known facts into another wider structure embracing them (for example, the writings of Pascal and Racine require insertion into the whole of the Jansenist movement). We must not forget, however, that the provisory knowledge one has of the facts of which one is a part is — to the precise extent that they constitute a wider element of the structure — one of the most important points of support for isolating this latter. (For example, one can use the writings of Pascal and Racine as a starting point for the hypothesis of the existence of an extremist Jansenism and the discovery of the latter as an essential means for understanding these works.)

To conclude, it remains for us to broach a problem that our readers have certainly taken into consideration by now. Let us assume that we are dealing with the insertion of works into a broader significant totality, a process which alone permits these structure and meaning to be isolated. Why have recourse to the rather distant totality of intellectual, social and economic movements? Why not do as most historians have explicitly or implicitly done, that is, limit oneself to texts bearing a significant totality much more closely and apparently bound to the work — the biography and psychology of the author?

The answer, seemingly paradoxical but actually rigorously justified, is simple: not for reasons of principle but for those of practicality and effectiveness in doing research.

Certainly, the theater of Racine and Pascal's *Pensées* are bound to the Jansenist movement only through the individual characteristics of their authors. Only an ideal study could in any case leap over an intermediary level of such importance. Unfortunately in practice, we do not have any solid and positive means of reconstituting the psychology of the individual. Most (and practically all) attempts of this sort are more or less intelligent and ingenious constructions which, however, have little connection with positive science. In the present state of the human sciences, it is much more the interpretation of the work that determines the impression one forms of the author rather than the inverse.

That is why it seems that at the present stage of scientific thought in the human sciences, one can formulate the following balance sheet:

(a) The concept of significant structure constitutes the principal instrument of research and the comprehension of most past and present facts. We use the word "most" consciously, given that certain sectors of social reality seem necessarily limited to the concept of structure, not that of significant structure.

(b) In every concrete analysis, the task of clarifying the specific significant structure governing the facts one intends to study comes up against two problems, both of which are difficult to resolve: the delimitation of the object, or if one wishes, the sector of reality corresponding to this significant structure, and the distinction within this sector between the essential and the accidental.

(c) The most important scientific procedure for resolving these problems is the insertion of the studied significant structures, even before they are completely isolated, into wider structures of which they are a part, a procedure that presumes a permanent *va et vient* from the part to the whole, and vice versa.

(d) If the concept of significant structure has a primary importance in the aggregate of the historical and social sciences, this importance is particularly reinforced in the area of philosophical, literary and artistic works. These are characterized not only by their *virtual* but also their *real* coincidence, or, more exactly, their near coincidence, with those rigorously coherent significant structures called world views.

(e) That is why literary criticism, as much as the history of philosophy, art and literature, could only surpass the relatively intelligent and original level of thought, thus acquiring a really positive status, to the extent that they take a structuralist orientation, attempting to relate the works they are studying to the basic structures of historical and social reality.

(f) Given the present limitations on our psychological knowledge, a similar study must today be placed first on the two levels of the immanent analysis of the work and its insertion into the historical and sociological structures of which it is a part. As for the intermediary structure constituted by the biography and the psychology of the philosopher, the artist or writer, even if one can in no way eliminate it in advance, it can, for the moment, constitute only a secondary instrument of research to be used with a good deal of distrust and skepticism.

(g) The number of historical situations and literary, philosophical and artistic works which correspond to them are incomparably greater than the number of world views (which explains, among other things, their rebirth). Such research will naturally have to be directed toward a typology of world views, which would constitute an invaluable instrument for research.

Yet, it is not a question of establishing from now on such a typology on psychological bases (as Karl Jaspers, for example, has tried to do). Such attempts bring into relief the area of "brilliant reflection," which has caused so much harm to science and which it is now, finally, time to surmount.

Like any serious scientific method, structuralism is not a universal key, but a working method that requires long and patient empirical studies. In itself it must be perfected and sharpened during the course of the studies.

Without doubt, there is a dialectic between empirical research and general ideas. Yet, one must not forget the priority of the former and its indispensable function in every scientific work worthy of the name.

4. The Social Structure and the
Collective Consciousness of Structures

Marxism was one of the first forms of structuralism. If we want to situate dialectical Marxism within the context of contemporary discussion, however, we must define it with respect to two other positions: positivism and non-genetic structuralism, which is becoming a sort of dominant ideology. On the basis of linguistics, this latter position takes in all of the psychological and historical sciences.

I would like to begin with an example. Some days ago, I had a discussion with a positivist sociologist. After his talk, I raised the objection that such subjects as "dictatorship" and "scandal" are not valid objects of sociological research, since they designate a classification that is too heterogeneous. Under the concept "dictatorship" one equally finds the regimes of Caesar, Hitler and those of Latin America. Such a method of research would be obliged to limit itself to the common traits of all these phenomena and would, therefore, be ineffective. The speaker answered: obviously, in any research one may choose the very general level over that of the specific. The difference between sociology and history lies precisely in this choice. Indeed, research usually chooses an intermediary level.

Now, it is exactly this thesis which seems questionable. There is a fundamental difference between this positivist position and the dialectical one. It is not true that historical and sociological research can choose any point whatsoever on a continuum extending from an extreme sociological generality to an extreme historical specificity. There is a precise point on this continuum which allows the researcher to isolate a typology. He can do so by studying a number of various scandals or dictatorships which are structurally related and, by studying their common traits, he can understand them better than if he had studied only one example of them. On the other hand, a researcher who would like to go further by encompassing heterogeneous facts would only contribute confusion.

The methodological problem is that of isolating the level of the object's structure so as to allow one to group together facts that are sufficiently related. In this way, they can clarify each other. At the same time, these very facts are also somewhat different from each other. The aim, then, is to isolate a structural law which is more than a simple description of a specific fact. One does not need some intermediate level between the extremes of the general and the particular, but a single and precise strategic level which avoids both the general abstractions peculiar to Auguste Comte's law of three stages and the descriptive monograph of the particular case.

I would also like to add at this point that historical reality is linked to a number of habits, activities and mental structures. Men living under similar conditions constitute social groups which elaborate a complex of habits and mental structures to resolve their problems. With these elaborations they are able to act in the world, but such habits and mental structures not only govern their behavior but also their intelligence, thought and emotions. These habits make up the very structural levels which I spoke about when discussing the most effective method of research, to the extent that they constitute elements which are linked together and structured into a whole. But one must not forget the very important fact that these structures (involving thought, behavior and emotions) create social realities as well: houses, roads, scandals, dictatorships, the relations of production, literary works, and the value judgments and theoretical concepts that one uses to study these various things. These mental habits, these psychological structures and behavioral structures are not individual facts. In other words, whenever we are dealing with historical and social phenomena (the type of production characteristic of the *ancien régime*, the capitalist mode of production, industrial production, economic crises or the tragedies of Racine), we can only make them sufficiently intelligible on a large scale (when historical and social facts are involved) and in their wholeness (when literary works are involved) by relating them to collective subjects. At the level of the truly important literary creation, where I work, we succeed, or nearly succeed, in accounting for the whole text as a significant unity.

The literary work has often been studied in its relation to an individual subject, the author. But the major difference between research of a genetic structuralist inspiration and traditional literary criticism lies in the fact that the former relates the work to a collective subject while the latter relates it to an individual one. More particularly, however, for genetic structuralism the collective subject constitutes a significant structure which is not entirely conscious. This significant structure always assumes the structuring of a collective subject which acts rationally or meaningfully within a given situation, in the midst of internally and externally inspired changes. Now, these changes can only be understood if one goes beyond the domain of this or that particular science, especially the one to which the object under study pertains.

I have been told, when raising the question of changes in social structures which could be the source of linguistic changes, that the structuration of society which acts upon language is not the problem of the linguist. If I want to understand the change from one literary structure to another, however, I must go beyond literature. I must take in a wider structuring process in order to understand the structuring process of the object studied.... Furthermore, a general law does not exist, only laws concerning tendencies.

The essential concept for history and sociology is that of "possible consciousness" which asserts a group's inclination toward an adequate and coherent consciousness, toward a coherence which a group rarely achieves except in moments of crisis and as an individual expression at the level of great cultural works.

In a recent book from the Althusserian school, Althusser poses a problem of method by saying: the major philosophical question of our time is the choice between Feuerbach and Spinoza. If I have understood correctly, according to him, Feuerbach asserts the existence of immanent meaning. If you seek this meaning you are an idealist, or you are Spinozian if you no longer seek meaning but only the mode of production. We are, moreover, not dealing with a historical Spinoza in this instance, or with the concrete reality of his thought. We are dealing only with the second mode of knowledge and a completely mechanistic

Spinoza. Basically, the alternative we are faced with is Pavlov or Hegel. Dialectical thought, at the scientific level where Marxism has situated it, rejects this alternative. It seeks simultaneously the meaning, the significant structure of the object being studied, as well as its production, its genesis, i.e., the functional need which has engendered it within a broader structure in which it fulfills a function.

To have a positive science, one must seek the structure of the object one is studying (depending on the case, a type of dictatorship, a great literary work, a revolutionary phenomenon or a migration). To do so, one must bring the object into as close a relationship as possible with other dictatorships, great literary works, revolutionary phenomena or migrations, with related structures and, at the same time, see it as a function of a broader structure (for example, language as a function of social communication). This communication is necessary and this need can, in certain instances, introduce changes in the structuring of language. I would say that in the history of the collective consciousness there are no sudden breaks. The reason for this is simple. Men have had to continue to communicate with each other; they have had to continue to produce in order to live. Then there is the ever-present need to organize their relationships, customs, etc. Men are always progressively adapting to their functional needs until a break occurs which testifies to the appearance of a new structure.

Characteristically, the statement that the fundamental problem of contemporary philosophy is the choice between Feuerbach and Spinoza is methodologically at the same level as the law of three stages. The concrete specificity of the thought of Feuerbach, Kant, Spinoza, Hegel and Marx is forgotten.

If we want to place ourselves at the level of the concrete, it is very important that we study a particular structuring process as a tendency within another englobing structure in which this process is made functional. The action of human groups, collective action, creates such structuring processes. Furthermore, these structures are historical.

I would like to end by taking up the problem of consciousness. . . . Human phenomena are unique; they are processes that always include consciousness. Within historical evolution, there are always moments of awareness, but it is not true that these moments are always appropriate to the given situation.

With respect to Cartesianism or Sartre's thought, one should know that meaningful and non-conscious behavior also exists (for example, a cat trapping a mouse, but also the greater part of collective and historical actions). Obviously, with regard to history and phenomena pertaining to the collective consciousness (phenomena which tend to adapt to reality and, thus, achieve a degree of equilibrium), moments of awareness correspond to these processes, although remaining relative. On the basis of a given situation, the awareness of groups is aimed at the problems of living. These moments of awareness are undoubtedly meaningful in themselves, but they are also implicitly a part of broader meanings. These latter usually escape the attention of these groups. There is a sort of mixture between the nonconscious and the progress of consciousness. As a result, the historian of ideas and the cultural creation cannot carry out a positive investigation by considering the interferences between these levels (the englobing structure, the immanent structure and the moments of awareness) unless he studies simultaneously the conscious and non-conscious elements.

In my essay, I have referred implicitly to Hegel and Marx. At the basis of dialectical thought there is a particular conception of structure which can be summarized in three points: (1) It is impossible to understand a structure without also considering its meaning and function; (2) This is so because structures are functional when related to their englobing structures and, finally, to human lives; (3) Men transform structures, create antagonisms and cause an old and superseded structure to be taken over by a new, functional and significant one. In the Hegelian and Marxist conception of structure, there are two fundamental ideas: the notion of the transindividual subject and that of genesis.

5. The Subject of the Cultural Creation

If I have chosen this theme, it is because it seems the most fitting in clarifying the profound similarities and the basic differences existing between the sociological and dialectical study of the cultural creation and the psychoanalytical approach.

In fact, even for the sociologist it is just as important not to ignore what psychoanalysis can contribute to the comprehension of man and the cultural creation as it is not to blur their differences for the purpose of reaching a sort of vague and eclectic serenity, which could only do harm to positive research.

Firstly, what are the common elements? I believe that Paul Ricoeur has already pointed them out this morning. Dialectical sociology and psychoanalysis both part from a common assertion: nothing is ever without meaning on the human level. As one often says of Hegelianism, this does not mean that dialectics is a panlogism. Given the contemporary development of formal logic, one could easily risk giving too strict a sense to the term. Perhaps it would be better to create a term derived not from "logic" but from "meaning," and speak of *pansignification*. This is an idea I have already had occasion to develop in a discussion with Paul Ricoeur in Montreal. One must remain aware of the fact that meaning does not begin with man or even less with thought and language. Nor, above all, is it always conscious.

Suppose we had a rather hungry cat in this room and a mouse were skirting the left wall. For the cat to concentrate on that wall and catch the mouse would be a perfectly meaningful action adapted both to the problem posed to the cat (that of appeasing its hunger and finding food) and to the context in which it is posed (that of a mouse going along the left wall toward which the cat must direct itself in order to catch it).

Now, although I do not know much about the psychology of animals, it is not in the least certain, nor even likely, that the cat is aware of the problem or the process he uses to resolve it. His behavior is not less meaningful because of that, however, in the sense that *meaning* stands for the implicit, biological and bodily resolution of a problem posed in a given situation.

No matter what the consciousness of the cat may be, what is important is the fact that for man, meaning has always been achieved through consciousness (true or false), communication, speech and language. Thus, we discover this meaningful consciousness every time we deal with either a present or a past human reality which has left sufficient traces and evidence for us to be able to study it.

Common to thinkers such as Hegel, Marx, Lukacs, Freud and I think I can add Piaget is the assertion that each time we find ourselves faced with a human action, a linguistic expression, a written sentence, or any sign of communication whatsoever, we are before a fragment of meaning *which will be revealed* once we succeed in integrating it into its total context.[1] This is so even if such a fragment of meaning is taken in its immediate form in which its rationality is not at first evident.

Further, whether it is a question of economics, the study of ideologies or political theories, the history of literature, philosophy, religion and scientific thought, or the analysis of dreams, neuroses, or slips of the tongue, the analyses of Marx and Freud are comparable. They both clarify the meaningful character (structural and functional) of such evidence or human behavior which at first appeared relatively, and at times completely, deprived of meaning. This is the first common element.

The second resides in the way in which Hegel, Marx, Lukacs and Freud manage to re-establish meaning on the basis of a fragment which in itself is not meaningful, or which appears at first to have a different meaning from that which dialectical or psychoanalytical research eventually brings to light.

For each of these thinkers, the way of reaching this point is by

---

1. This statement also includes biological behavior because at the human and symbolic level the biological itself becomes meaningful, or, as Sartre said, it becomes "consciousness-of-itself" and eventually reflective consciousness.

integrating the object studied into a relatively broader totality called structure, social life, a network of images or an unconscious psychism. Let me add that in this perspective the notion of polysemism, which has been spoken about so much during this colloquium, becomes perfectly acceptable. It simply means the possibility of validly integrating the object studied into many different structures, both at the level of consciousness and that of history. Perhaps one could even include the biological level here, though this is beyond my competence.

The third point in common is the idea that structures are not invariable and permanent but constitute the outcome of a genetic process. One can understand the meaningful character of a structure only from an aggregate of actual situations in which the subject, *already structured by its previous development*, tries to change old structures in order to answer problems posed by these situations. Eventually, these efforts of the subject will gradually modify its actual structure to the degree that external influences, or even the behavior of the subject and its action upon the surrounding world, will have a transforming effect and pose new problems.

Briefly, the thought both of Freud and Marx is a genetic structuralism (of course, these two names have a general value here and stand for all positive and dialectical sociology as well as Freudian psychoanalysis). This said, however, one must also insist on the differences separating Marxism from psychoanalysis.

Firstly, these seem to me to be situated at the point I propose to deal with today — that of the subject of human behavior and, thence, the subject of meaning and meaningful language; and within this behavior and language, that of the distinction between the subject of libidinal behavior and the subject of historical action and of the cultural creation which is part of it.

The essential difference between dialectical sociology and Freudian thought appears to reside in the way they conceive the subject. In fact, for two complementary reasons Freud has always seen the subject as an individual. This he has done, first, to the degree that he is still situated within Enlightenment thought,

---

2. Among other things, this explains his deep hostility toward religion, which Ricoeur spoke about this morning (an extremely common attitude of Enlightenment philosophers) and the short-circuiting of reason, owing to which he reduced religion to an illusion and an ideology.

which for several centuries has been the dominant form of thought in the Western world and which has always been based on the individual, under one form or another. Whether the Cartesian or Husserlian *Cogito* or the sensations or formal propositions of the empiricists, it has always been the individual who was seen as the only possible subject of action or thought.

This at times led to forms both as paradoxical and revelatory as that which I have cited in one of my books: a third or fourth grade grammar in which one could read, as if it were a matter of an obvious truth, that " 'I' is a pronoun that does not have a plural; 'we' signifies 'I' and 'you'." For Enlightenment thought, and for Freud, there are only individuals. The subject is always an 'I.'

Freud has reinforced this individualist position in his great discoveries, especially that of the unconscious. Even when he has gone beyond Enlightenment thought in approaching a dialectical conception of the personality, he faced the biological aspect first, or that immediately derived from it — sexuality, or desire, or the more appropriate term *libido* which avoids the possibility of confusing this term (desire) with Hegelian terminology.

Even if the structure of the *libido* is not particularly genital (and Freud was the first to discover and teach that it certainly is not) I believe that one can define it quite rigorously by the fact that it exclusively embraces pulsions. From the biological point of view, the subject of such pulsions is an individual for whom other individuals are objects and, more precisely, objects of satisfaction or obstacles (for example, the father and mother in the Oedipus complex).

This said, however, it is evident that once these tendencies are integrated into a personality capable of symbolic thought and language, they become more complex and acquire new characteristics. The subject learns to think of itself as an "I" and integrates this construction into its reflective consciousness. At this point, then, it can make the "I" into an object of pulsions. Thus develops the phenomenon of narcissism, a specifically human aspect, and the various subsequent characteristics at the level of the human subject. According to us, though, this is only a secondary factor with respect to the cultural creation — one of the most important particularities of the high points of the collective consciousness: the identity of the subject and the object.

Whatever the reasons may be, however, it is a fact that Freudian analyses of the cultural creation are a kind of rigorous transposition of analyses of individual behavior and the individual *libido*.

Structuralist psychology is by now well established. Still, the practice of transposing the individual subject from the biological and libidinal domain to that of social life and cultural works appears very problematical. I fear that it fails to question the positive and scientific interest of these analyses.

Before broaching the essence of the problem, however, I would like to recall that some of the important and contestable particularities of Freudian thought seem to follow from this position. I will settle for one of them: the absence of the category of the future.

The future of the individual, in fact, is limited. It ceases with death and it would be difficult to make it one of the fundamental categories of individualist thought.

Further, the disappearance of the category of totality in individualism also involves, as an afterthought, the disappearance of the idea of time and its replacement by two other equivalent and atemporal categories, namely the *moment* and *eternity*. It is not an accident that this atemporality characterizes the two major rationalist thinkers: Descartes and Spinoza. Similarly, one could show that although the political involvement of Enlightenment thinkers in the 18th century led them to struggle for a better future, they had difficulty in rooting this idea in their systems, often conceived under an atemporal form.

Further, there is nothing surprising in the fact that Freud's thought, in spite of its genetic character, ignores the future and seems to develop into a two-dimensional temporality: the present and the past, with a clear dominance of the latter. If I am not mistaken, the word "future" is found only once in the title of one of his books, *The Future of an Illusion,* which demonstrates that this illusion does not have a *future*.

Let us return, however, to the problem that concerns us and which Freud himself raises in *Civilization and its Discontents*.

There he observes that the free satisfaction of libidinal tendencies, which take as their object the first beings which the child encounters, namely his father and mother, would result in the creation of three autonomous groups and would hinder any formation of a wider society.

Men have created wider societies, however; and to do so, they have forbidden the satisfaction of the most intense libidinal drives: precisely those corresponding to the Oedipus complex. The prohibition of incest is one of the most widespread and general social institutions that we know. Freud asks how one can know who has been able to get men freely to accept so serious and painful a frustration in order to create social life and civilization. He affirms that this is one of the crucial problems of the human sciences, for the solution of which scientists even now could not formulate a serious hypothesis. This reply, which puts into question Freudian individualism, Marxism had formulated a long time ago.

With the development of the symbolic function, language and communication, the entirely new and revolutionary means of satisfying the other basic need of man (beside the *libido*), the preservation of life, had appeared. We will use the term "mastery over nature" to characterize the kind of behavior corresponding to this second need.

Despite the development and modifications brought about by consciousness, the symbolic function and language, the *libido* always remained individual. On the other hand, the kind of behavior corresponding to the need to master nature changed completely in order to better the conditions of life. Indeed, with communication and language, there came about the possibility of a division of labor. The latter, in turn, acted upon the symbolic function. This is what Piaget has called the shock of change, which generated something completely new and until now unknown: *the subject made up of several individuals*.

If I lift a very heavy table with my friend John, it is neither I nor John who lifts it. The subject of this action, in the most rigorous sense of the word, is constituted by John and me (and, of course, for other actions one should add a much greater number of individuals). That is why relations between John and me are not subject-object relations, as in the domain of the *libido* or the Oedipus complex. Nor are they intersubjective as individualist philosophers think, who take individuals to be absolute subjects. I prefer to designate the relations between John and me by a neologism, whereby they are termed *intrasubjective*, i.e., those relations between individuals each of whom is a partial element of the true subject of action.

In order to be able to lift the table together, we must be able to name it and set up a whole series of other things. It is, then, necessary that there be theory. Further, whatever will be said on the theoretical level must remain bound to behavior which takes for its object both the surrounding natural world and other human groups. In this domain the subject will be transindividual and all communication between John and me with respect to lifting the table remains communication within the subject, i.e., *intrasubjective.*

It is here that the fundamental break between dialectical sociology and psychoanalysis seems to be located. Because Freud, who discovered the domain of unconscious drives and the behavior aimed at satisfying them, has also naturally seen those drives created, or at least assimilated, by society. The satisfaction of these drives is essentially bound to consciousness, the domain of behavior directly or indirectly oriented toward the mastery of nature and cultural works.

Unfortunately, he has not recorded the change in the nature of the subject, which is established in the passage from one level of drives to the other, and that is why he has always connected them to an individual subject. Quite characteristically, he has categorized them under the global term of "*Ichtriebe*," i.e., "pulsions of the ego." On the contrary, what characterizes the appearance of man, the birth of civilization and, with it, the appearance of consciousness and the division of labor, is the development of a sector of life and behavior peculiar to the transindividual subject. And here one should remember that this subject acts not only upon the natural world but also upon other men or groups of men, which then make up the object of its thought and action.

The true opposition is not, as Freud thought, between the

pulsions of the Id (the individual subject controlled by the unconscious and the biological) and those of the Ego (an individual subject as well, but directed by the conscious and the socialized). It is located between the pulsions of the Id and those structuring the consciousness of a being who, while remaining biologically an individual, is also a conscious and socialized being representing only a *partial element of a subject which transcends him.*

We may add that in this perspective there is no difficulty in admitting that energy which is spent in social behavior finds its origins in the transformation of libidinal drives. The true or false character of this assertion is a problem for psychology.

We must stress that the conception of the subject as individual or transindividual is not a simple terminological problem, but a decisive one for all research in the human sciences. Indeed, it is just as much a matter of understanding the subject behind conscious behavior, which renders the latter, even if only partially conscious, intelligible.

For psychoanalysis, this intelligibility is always related to an individual subject. Social behavior is only secondary and derived; in the last analysis, its intelligibility is imposed from without, even if later interiorized.

For dialectical thought, on the other hand, behavior is made intelligible by relating it to a collective subject. In this case the individual subject is subordinate and secondary in explaining behavior, since it presents such irrational phenomena as madness, dreams or even the Freudian slip.

Of course, we are not faced with a collective consciousness which is situated outside individual consciousnesses, there being no consciousness apart from that of individuals. Only, some individuals find themselves in relations which are *intrasubjective* rather than intersubjective and, thus, constitute the subject of all thought and action which is social and cultural.

In short, the meaning which psychoanalysis discovers in such apparently absurd human manifestations as the slip, dreams and neuroses is based on a different conception of the subject than that of sociological analysis, which discovers objective meaning behind apparent meanings or the seeming absence of meaning in social, historical and cultural facts. An individual subject coincides with the biological subject in the first case, a transindividual subject (plural, if you wish) in the second.

In order to avoid any misunderstanding, we should add that in certain conditions the plural subject, responsible for elaborating theory and world views, can also elaborate an individualist view. In other words, the latter is not any less collective than all the other forms of thought. In being isolated on his island, Robinson Crusoe is no less collective a creation than the views and forms of thought which deny that the individual is a reality.

Obviously, this form of intrasubjective community, which I have described to you in order to simplify the relation between two persons who propose to lift a table, is idyllic and far removed from actual social reality.

It serves, nevertheless, to illustrate the problem. I do not have time to insist upon the many forms of social pathology first analyzed by Marx, Marxist thinkers and many other sociologists and historians; notably, Adorno and the Frankfurt School. . . .

Concrete analyses of the forms of social pathology will be needed, especially with respect to contemporary Western societies where such phenomena as reification, the replacement of the qualitative and human by the quantitative and the pathologies of bureaucratic and technocratic organization exist. Whatever these forms of social pathology may be, however, they are basically different from the pathological forms of the *libido*. Indeed, the first are pathologies of the transindividual subject, of cooperation and the division of labor, the second are pathologies of the individual.

Here I come to the essential question which I should like to put to Ricoeur. I completely agree with him when he points out that all genetic structuralisms, whether psychoanalysis or dialectical sociology, are constantly threatened by the same danger: that of reduction, of *only*. This painting is *only* the expression of a libidinal desire, the work of Valéry is *only* the ideological expression of petty-bourgeois thought.

I also agree with him in believing that forms of genetic structuralism must explain how a starting point has been gone beyond in order to end with a superior complex creation, and not how this creation is reduced to the starting point. But I should like to ask him if, insofar as it reduces everything to the *libido* and the individual subject, psychoanalytic thought, while the *least reductive in its own domain*, does not necessarily become reductive when it broaches the cultural creation. I should like to ask him if the possibility of referring the latter to a collective subject will not always be missing for it, and if society does not remain simply the milieu through which the individual subject is expressed. Now, I think that is one of the most problematic and empirically insufficient points of the psychoanalytic perspective. Another problem, connected to the one we are now dealing with, was raised in...private conversation.

What are the relations between interpretation and explanation? I think I can give you an answer. This is an important question which, it seems to me, has been dealt with for the most part in a highly contestable way. Indeed, as the competence of the casual physico-chemical sciences, *explanation* has been artificially opposed to *interpretation*, proper to the human sciences, which should be the area of participation, dialogue and, at times, the affections.

For dialectical thought, the problem is posed differently. Comprehension is an intellectual process:[3] it is the description of the specificity and essence of a meaningful structure. To bring to light the meaningful character of a work of art, a philosophical work or a social process, and the immanent sense of their structuring process is to *understand* them by showing that they are structures that have their own coherence. To *explain* is to locate these elements in wider structures that encompass them. *Explanation always concerns a structure that encompasses and goes beyond the structure studied.*

An essential question, then, arises in our problematic: in order to interpret a dream, to discover its significance, the psychoanalyst can never stop at an immanent interpretation, at a simple clarification of its structure. He must have recourse to unconscious drives, must insert the dream into something wider which is not simply its manifest contents and must account for the process of transformation. The question is raised: why cannot one understand and interpret dreams as one could, at the most,

---

3. This does not mean a purely theoretical attitude to the extent that every theoretical attitude is both theoretical and practical.

understand and interpret Racine's *Phèdre* or Aeschylus' *Orestes?*
Yesterday I said that it seemed absurd to admit the existence of
an unconscious Orestes. He is none other than the literary
character certified by the text and does not have an existence
outside it. Now, as we have just said, psychoanalysis cannot
interpret a dream without going beyond its overt content, i.e.,
without having recourse to explanation. In sociological analysis,
of course, I nearly always go beyond the text, but it is to *explain*
and not to comprehend it, while one is *obliged* to explain a
dream in order to discover its meaning.

The reason is that by itself, the dream does not make up a
meaningful structure and, as a conscious manifestation, is only
an *element* of such a structure (biological and individual), while
social logic creates meaningful structures having a relative
autonomy and its own meaning. Obviously, there is an
explanation of the dream as there is for conscious structures.
What distinguishes one from the other, though, is their respective
positions on a continuum which goes from the purely biological
(with no meaning beyond explanation) to the major cultural
work (in principle susceptible to an autonomous understanding
different from explanation). In practical research, it is true,
explanation always helps in understanding, and vice versa.

That explains why each time we wish to locate the dream in
relation to conscious logic, i.e., to *interpret* it, we must refer to
the unconscious as an *explanatory* factor of the dream
formations. We must find the latent meaning, due to the need to
explain the distortions of meaning in relation to social logic.
Briefly, what distinguishes cultural works from dreams is that the
former are located on a level of meaning related to the collective
subject. Not that psychoanalysis cannot find libidinal meaning at
that level, because there is no collective consciousness outside
individual consciousnesses. Every individual consciousness is
composed both of libidinal elements, the subject of which is
individual, and conscious elements, which are thrown into relief
at the level of cultural creations and for which the subject is
transindividual.

Naturally, there are not two separate sectors within consciousness. In this interpenetration, though, it can happen that the
collective element succeeds in keeping its autonomy as well as its

own law, and thus generates meaning in relation to the trans-individual subject which acts, works and elaborates the culture. In this case the elements of individual satisfaction can enter into consideration only to the extent that they are adapted to this logic without modifying it. These elements will be able to account for the fact that it is precisely Racine the individual who has written the plays we know and not someone else. The meaning of these plays, the necessary use of the absolute, the deaf characters, and the spectators whom the hero interprets according to an insoluble contradiction and the distance separating the tragic character from their demands, is a transposition of categories elaborated by the Jansenist group. The only valid and valuable contribution that psychoanalysis can make is that of knowing why these categories are manifested with a particular force in Racine and how it happens that they have coincided with the author's personal problems to such an extent that he has succeeded in giving a particularly coherent form to the current tendencies of the entire Jansenist group. If, on the other hand, there is no coincidence between the individual and intrasubjective, if individuals succeed in upsetting the logic and structure of the collective meaning, then we shall progressively pass from the work of Racine to the average consciousness, and at the other extreme, to dreams and pathology.

Now, to the extent that psychoanalysis tries to connect the whole of consciousness to the I, the individual, and the libidinal, it is fatally led to efface the differences between these various kinds of expression in abandoning every criterion which would permit it to distinguish the sick person from the genius.

When the psychoanalyst finds himself before a piece of writing or a painting, in conformity with his very method he locates them on the same level as the sick or alienated person.... From his viewpoint he is right. Most likely, the cultural creation and the drawing of a madman function in the same way for him. The psychoanalyst is probably right also in maintaining that Racine expressed certain unconscious and libidinal desires in writing his plays.

It is only when libidinal and unconscious drives are expressed in the work without distorting the latter's meaning that they reinforce the cultural value — at the literary juncture — of the latter.

One must constantly recall a basic assertion of genetic structuralist sociology: the meaningful (collective) coherence of works of art, far from being more personal than the thought and writings of average persons, on the contrary, attains a much higher degree of social representativeness.

Every time we approach an important cultural text or a historical event, we find ourselves before an object of study in which the transindividual subject, or the collective subject if you will, is expressed at a much higher level of coherence than that attained by the consciousness of average individuals (mine or yours, for example), i.e., at a level where positive study can abstract the individual factor. This is not to say that libidinal satisfaction may not have existed or made up an important link in the genesis of the work. It is, however, particularly difficult to grasp and contributes only very little to an understanding of the object one wishes to study.[4]

I recently had a discussion about this which I should like to recall here, because it has helped me to avoid a misunderstanding. At the time of an exposé on sociological aesthetics, during the course of which I had mentioned the example of 17th-century French tragedy, some of my listeners who were historians of literature raised an unexpected objection:

"All this is very well, and we readily agree, but can your sociological categories grasp the aesthetic fact and would it not be necessary, to do so, to add them to specifically literary categories?"

Now, I never intended to use sociological categories for the *understanding of a work*. The latter's aesthetic quality depends firstly upon its richness, its meaningful coherence and upon the coherence between its universe and its form, in the strict sense of the word. In order to bring this internal meaning and coherence to light, however, I must employ *explanatory* processes which imply its insertion into a wider structure, i.e., a social structure. In doing so, I in no way wish to find sociological elements in the work. The latter is nothing other than a text having, or not having, a coherent structure. Once again, I recall what I said

---

4. For example, this was the case when we tried to understand the tragic plays of Racine, Pascal's *Pensées* and the Jansenist movement to which both were bound.

yesterday: when interpreting *Orestes*, one can undoubtedly have recourse to explanatory processes by inserting it into an enclosing structure, into the psychology of Aeschylus or into Athenian society, for example, but one does not have the right to add a line or a word to the text. The character of Orestes can, then, eventually be explained by the *unconscious of Aeschylus* or by the social structures of Athens. One could not, however, attribute its own unconscious to it, as one will not find a sentence in the text which explicitly affirms the existence of the latter, and still less could one introduce sociological categories into the text.

In short, in cases where there is a predominance of libidinal meaning, the researcher is obliged to resort to explanation in order to be able to interpret it. In the case of cultural works, interpretation and explanation are complementary processes, mutually facilitated during the course of research but, still, are different processes.

The individual could not penetrate the work of art without weakening or destroying it, except so far as it is integrated into a collective meaning. It happens that when the psychoanalyst approaches the study of his work by seeking individual meanings in it, he will undoubtedly find them there, and at times in very great number, but nearly always by cutting it into pieces and leaving aside its total structure and essential problematic.

When one is dealing with Michelangelo's Moses, or the smiles of Saint Ann and Mary in the picture "The Holy Family," the important thing is not that of knowing what in the life of Leonardo, in his relations with the pope and his father has led him to paint them in a certain way — because similar libidinal relations could have existed at another time and in another society — but what he has done that this expression of individual desires has been able to be inserted into a structure and into a work of art which, at the level of what is painted, is very meaningful and coherent. Relations that are similar to those between Pascal and his sister Jacqueline exist, perhaps, by the thousands. It is at a certain moment and in a certain context that this relation proves to be particularly favorable for expressing in an extremely coherent way a world view elaborated at Port Royal with Saint-Cyran and, beyond, within a particular social group, the nobility of the robe in France.

This leads us to pose a particularly important problem: that of the nature of aesthetic satisfaction, since, evidently, this satisfaction includes an element of pleasure. A few minutes ago, someone asked me, "What do you do with the pleasure felt when one is before a work of art? In spite of everything, it is of the same order at the one Freud speaks about with respect to the libido."

Yes and no, since each time, it is a matter of the relation between psychoanalysis and dialectics. Yes, to the extent that a strict bond exists between the social function of the work of art and the individual function of the imaginary, the dream and madness, such as has been described by Freud. In fact, both are born from the inadequacy of the subject's aspirations in relation to reality. In order to support the frustrations this imposes upon him, man is obliged to compensate for them by an imaginary creation which, moreover, favors its insertion into the surrounding world in as much as one is dealing with a normal and not a pathological psychology.

No, to the extent that at the individual level, these frustrations nearly always concern an object (and most often a human being functioning as the object) which the individual subject has not been able to possess. Inversely, at the level of the transindividual subject, aspiration does not, or at least does not primarily, concern an object, but a meaningful coherence, frustration being constituted by the fact that reality imposes upon each of us some degree of incoherence and a number of compromises.

This results not only from the relationship between the collective subject and its surrounding world, but also from the very structure of this subject, composed of individuals pertaining to a large number of diverse social groups and in whose consciousness (Freud has sufficiently shown) libidinal elements intervene. Thus, these individuals make up mixtures as well as the transindividual subject of a group, which tends toward coherent meaning without ever succeeding in effectively attaining it.

The most important function of artistic and literary creations on the imaginary level appears to be to contribute coherence which men are frustrated in achieving in real life, exactly as on the individual level dreams, deliria and the imaginary procure the object or its substitute, which the individual has never been able actually to possess.

Still, there is a great difference between the coherence of a conscious structure bound to a collective subject, a coherence not always reducible to an explicit meaning, and the latent coherence of a libidinal structure bound to an individual subject.

I have already said that in both cases the imaginary creation has as its function the compensation of a frustration. Only, in the case of the individual subject and the libidinal frustrations studied by Freud, it is a matter of turning to the censor of consciousness, of surreptitiously introducing into the latter elements which it refused to admit and had repressed.

In the case of cultural creations, on the other hand, the search for coherence makes up an explicit or implicit tendency of the consciousness which is not at all repressed. Creation here reinforces consciousness in its immanent tendencies while the *libido* usually tries to get around it and introduce foreign elements contrary to its nature.

This difference, though, is not made to astonish us, granted consciousness is strictly bound to the collective subject or, if you will, to the transindividual subject. On the contrary, it appears in the libidinal domain only to the extent that when the libidinal is present in man, it is obliged to incorporate this general element of human nature (the existence of consciousness) by trying to maintain its own structure, by assimilating at least some conscious elements into its own needs.[5]

Of course, unconscious elements are almost always integrated into the coherence of a global structure, whether it be by deforming it through dreams, madness or Freudian slips, or by preserving in it its explicit and clear structure while adding an overdetermination of the libidinal type.

In this last case, along with satisfactions of the transindividual type provided by cultural creations, there are also individual

---

5. Still, when speaking about the transindividual or collective subject, it is always necessary to mention that one is dealing, not with what the Durkheimian school meant by the term, i.e., a collective consciousness located outside, above or alongside the individual consciousness, but, on the contrary, with a collective subject in the sense given it this morning by M. Bastide, i.e., relations between men and others in a situation in which the other is not the object of thought, desire or action, but is part of the subject and is in the process of elaborating a position or of performing an action in common with me.

satisfactions and pleasures common to everyone. . . . When this is produced, the reception of the work proves to be favorable. For a work to be so, though, this coincidence is not necessary. Each particular case must be investigated by itself.

It is important to underline that when one is dealing with the interpretation of a cultural work in its specifically cultural aspects, the system of thought which binds it to the individual and libidinal subject could play only a secondary role and could even be entirely eliminated. This is especially so when it is an important work. It is also necessary to add that, given the extreme difficulty of knowing the individual consciousness — especially when it concerns a writer whom one cannot spend several months analyzing or who died several centuries ago — it is particularly the work and its transindividual coherence that contribute the decisive elements in our understanding of the author — to the extent that the sociologist succeeds in revealing this coherence. This was the case during the course of our research on Pascal and Racine.

We may add tht the study of the conflicts and interpretations between intrasubjective and libidinal coherence poses another problem upon which the Frankfurt School has particularly insisted (but which, I think, should be studied more concretely, should be more historically situated, especially both within and without the context of contemporary society): that of knowing to what extent transindividual coherence, with all that it involves on the practical, economic, social, political and cultural levels, generates important frustrations in the personal life of the subject. According to Freud, who has said so in a rather categorical way, one knows that all social life implies frustrations of the libido, so that there will always be a cultural malaise. This remains extremely general, however, because as Marcuse, Adorno and their colleagues have seen so well, these frustrations can have a relatively intense character, especially being unequally distributed among individuals and social groups. It is a fact that they are not equitably and homogeneously distributed among the different social classes.

Now, the question today is that of knowing to what degree the high technical level attained by advanced industrial societies would allow these frustrations to be reduced to the minimum for each individual, if the social order were more effectively organized. It is also a question of knowing to what degree the concrete forms that contemporary society has taken, notably technocratic society, organized capitalism, are at the root of the frustrations that most people today accept.

Whatever it may be, I do not believe it is enough to say that work can become a pleasure and that today, given the high standard of living, one could effectively confer on it this gamey aspect. As Bastide has said this morning, current social organization unquestionably has a tendency to efface the individual within the transindividual subject, in organizing a kind of spontaneous and implicit brainwork.

Further, the most important practical problem of our time is precisely that of knowing in what direction to act, what attitude to take in order to contribute a different orientation to social evolution from the one it seems in the process of taking spontaneously. I am referring to an orientation which would permit one to change the present tendency toward the suppression of the qualitative element and the human personality, even though the standard of living and the people's buying power have considerably increased. This then creates a situation which I once characterized as the paradoxical element on the cultural level. We risk having a large number of university graduates and illiterate professors...and a social structure able effectively to assure harmonious development both for the libidinal side of the subject (which today has the right and the potentiality to achieve much greater and more intense satisfactions than those which earlier societies, living under the pressure of penury and scarcity, were able to offer him) and for the intrasubjective and socialized personality....

Both in psychoanalysis and in sociology, however, this leads us to the problem of what attitude to assume toward contemporary society and the alternatives still available. As you well know, this is a very important problem which I do not want to underestimate, but it is not the theme of today's talk.

To conclude, I would like to add a remark to the fine paper we heard this morning by Roger Bastide. Indeed, I am not sure that everything may have been said when he emphasizes that the replacement of the quantitative by the qualitative ends up in a return to archaic values. I am not sure that it is *only* a matter of archaism here and not, on the contrary, of the future and innovation. Human needs are by nature bound to the qualitative aspect of objects. Thus, it is possible that the reappearance in men's *consciousness* of qualitative relations with things and with other human beings may, at least from the formal viewpoint, be both a return to archaic values and a real and essential orientation toward the possibilities of human development in the future.

Finally, to conclude this talk, I should like to use a particularly suggestive example. I have read in Freud's remarks on Leonardo that the construction of the flying machine is closely bound to libidinal symbolism which psychoanalysis often finds in the dreams of its patients during the course of therapeutic activity. Not being a psychoanalyst, I cannot discuss this, and I wish to admit the technical validity of such an assertion. What interests me is the hypothesis which follows: each time you see someone actually or imaginatively constructing a flying machine, and notably in Leonardo's case since he imagined such a machine long before it was technically realizable, it is a libidinal element which predominates and which, finally, ended in the development of the contemporary technique of aviation.

It seems to me that even if we accept the three starting points of this analysis — namely:

(1) The fact that men often have dreams in which they see themselves flying;

(2) The fact that these dreams are bound to certain libidinal drives and constitute sublimated satisfactions;

(3) The fact that Leonardo imagined a flying machine and that, since, the technique of flying has taken on a very great importance in human society and in men's lives —

even if we admit these, one could not admit the bond that Freud and psychoanalysis try to establish.

Perhaps — if Freud is right — men have always dreamed they could fly. At the time when Leonardo constructed his models of flying machines, however, we were at a specific stage in the development of the sciences and technology, and flying machines were for him only one attempt among many others. It would be difficult to separate in a clear way the model of the flying machine having a libidinal meaning from all his other attempts which, for the historian of such technology and of the sciences, have an absolutely homologous character.

In other words, for every attempt to locate this work in the history of scientific and technical thought, Freud's analysis and the bond that he tried to establish have a secondary and even negligible character, unless it is unnecessary to deny the existence of the latter. If we wish to understand the actual and objective nature of the phenomenon, we must put ourselves, above all, on the level of the historical and transindividual subject.

This example seems particularly pertinent to illustrate the problematic that I wanted to deal with in this conference.

In conclusion, I think that it is necessary both to accept and to reject psychoanalysis; to accept it in every case on the level of the individual psychological study, of clinical therapy, and also to leave it a considerable place in the analysis of the psychological processes of the cultural creation, but also to avoid any attempt to connect the objective meaning of this creation to an individual subject, a process that must necessarily (for methodological reasons) lead to a dangerous reduction, and even to the complete effacement of this meaning. When I speak of subjective meaning, it would perhaps be more worthwhile to say the *specific* meaning; indeed, it is a matter of the literary meaning of literary works, the pictorial meaning of paintings, the philosophical meaning of philosophical systems, the theological meaning of theological writings, etc.

6. Theses on the Use of the Concept "World View"
in the History of Philosophy

(1) By 'world view' we mean a *coherent* and *unitary* perspective concerning man's relationships with his fellow men and with the universe. Since the thought of individuals is rarely coherent and unitary, a world view rarely corresponds to the actual thought of a particular individual.

Thus, a world view is not a given empirical reality, but a conceptual instrument for doing research; an extrapolation constructed by the historian which, however, is not arbitrary, since it is founded on the structure of the real thought of individuals.

(2) Philosophical thought is a *conceptual* attempt to respond to basic human problems. Now, the responses that a thinker gives to these problems are not independent from each other. A link exists among the ways of considering the most diverse realities, among answers to questions entirely foreign to each other, which shapes thought into a coherent totality or, conversely, into an eclectic assemblage of scattered elements. In the first instance this thought is philosophical; in the second it is not.

(3) The value of a scientific theory is established only in relation to its correspondence to reality. Philosophical systems, on the other hand, require at least two complementary criteria in order to be evaluated. A system is valid not only because it implies true affirmations, but also because it is the coherent conceptual expression of a fundamental human reality. One cannot recognize any truth in it, or agree with it in any way, if one disowns or underestimates its philosophical importance.

(4) Except in the particular case of rationalist philosophy, this coherence is not *logical* but *human*. The internal links that connect Pascal's concept of a gamble to his epistemology, those

that join Kant's practical postulates to the whole of his philosophy, without being logical in the strictest sense of the word, are no less necessary than the links uniting the ontological argument to the affirmation of the external world's existence in Cartesian thought.

(5) The history of philosophy, therefore, must consider the systems it studies as expressions of different and complementary world views, without thereby renouncing the second equally important criterion for its study, that of the truth value of the thought to be studied.

(6) The distinction between philosophy, literature and art, one which evidences their relationships as well as the differences that separate them into autonomous domains, consists in this: all three of these forms of spiritual creation are expressions of world views translated into three radically different languages.

Philosophy is expressed through general concepts, while the writer and artist create an imaginary universe of individual beings and things. Thus, Pascal reflects on *death* and *passion* while Racine creates Phèdre's death and passion for Hyppolite.

(7) Any attempt to make world views depend upon individuals seems insufficient to us. This is because they are common to the most diverse people, such as the philosopher, the writer and the artist, or to individuals as different as Kant and Psacal, Descartes and Malebranche.

(8) World views are *historical* and *social* facts. They are totalities of ways of thinking, feeling and acting which in given conditions are imposed on men finding themselves in a similar economic and social situation, that is, imposed on certain social groups. Through these latter, it is clear that new world views do not appear all at once. Nor are they generated by an isolated individual's intuition, no matter how enlivening it may be. Slow, gradual transformations of an old mentality are needed in order to permit the new to be established and to overcome the first. Similar transformations can only very rarely be the work of one man because the emotional, intellectual and material difficulties which it would be necessary for him to overcome far surpass the forces of an isolated individual. Many efforts oriented in the same direction and often extended over several generations are necessary for the creation of a world view. In a word, a social

movement is needed, and the philosopher is only the first to translate in a nearly consequential way the new problems posed to the people of a particular society and the answers that they prepare to give; *the first to make this new world view into a coherent totality on the level of conceptual thought.*

(9) Every attempt to connect world views to nationalities appears insufficient. Indeed, the entire philosophical thought of one nation undoubtedly presents common traits, but these are too few and too general to characterize the essential content of a philosophical system.

Precisely because national thought (French, English, German, etc.) embraces different philosophical systems, one could never connect world views, which constitute the essential contents of particular philosophical systems, to it. On the other hand, the same world view can be expressed in the thought of philosophers of different nationalities.

Likewise, the joining of world views to generations is neither comprehensible in itself nor factually confirmed. One could never be satisfied with a few concordances resulting simply from the fact that world views and generations both follow in the same chronological moment. Such a position, moreover, would render the succession of philosophical systems entirely irrational and contingent.

(10) It is, therefore, necessary to link world views to relatively homogeneous social groups, in similar historical situations or presenting certain similarities, world views constituting an aggregate of humanly coherent responses in relation to these situations.

Concrete studies have shown that during a determinate historical period (a period which one must delimit in a precise way with other equally concrete studies) social classes in Eastern Europe have made up — and perhaps still do — such groups; the passing of a particular social class from one world view to another, corresponding to basic historical transformations or to transformations in its relations with other social classes.

The usefulness of the concept world view derives not only from its importance for the understanding of a philosophical system as a meaningful and coherent fact, but also from its fundamental importance for the understanding of the historical functions of each philosophical system, and for every attempt to make an immanent critique of it, this being possible only in the perspective:

(a) of starting points and the system's internal coherence;

(b) of its conformity to the reality which it is trying to understand and explain.

(12) Such an immanent critique should distinguish:

(a) the analysis of the individual inconsistencies of the thinker owing to the survival of old forms of thought concerning a number of subordinate points, or owing to concessions before the established powers (church, state, etc.);

(b) the analysis of inconsistencies owing to the desire of the thinker to avoid too flagrant differences between his thought and the reality he hopes to understand;

(c) the analysis of the internal limits of the world view under examination, limits which one can isolate only by presuming that the thinker is at a level of extreme coherence, which is rarely the case in reality.

(13) In every case the number of world views is more limited than that of the historical situations which the various social groups in the course of history find, or will find, themselves to be in. Almost all of these views, however, have been able to express different and at times even opposite social and economic situations. One need think only of Platonism, which, though aristocratic in ancient Greece and still so in the Augustinianism of the middle ages, later became, in the hands of Galileo and Descartes, one of the chief means of philosophically expressing the Third Estate's opposition to the aristocracy.

This phenomenon allows one to explain, among other things, the renaissances; but it also poses one of the major problems of the philosophy of history: that of the typology of world views.

(14) Since world views articulate the different possibilities of human reaction to the infinite multiplicity of concrete historical situations, the history of philosophy (like that of literature and art) constitutes one of the most crucial ways toward the elaboration of a philosophical anthropology.

To establish a typology of world views, therefore, is to bring about an essential contribution to the understanding of man and humanity. This typology, nevertheless, can only be the outcome of many concrete and partial historical analyses. In no case has one the right to construct it in advance, before these analyses have been undertaken and completed.

If there is a human essence, it can be known only through the actual study of humanity, living and acting, in other words, in the final analysis, through history, of which the history of philosophy makes up an integral and inseparable part.

7. Sociological and Cultural Denunciation

As for the title of my essay, permit me to say that it was not chosen by me. If I have accepted it, it is because it seemed somehow suitable for introducing one of my essential preoccupations concerning our contemporary societies.

To clarify my intentions immediately, I will divide my essay into two parts: the first will be dedicated to an analysis of the theatrical works of Genet and Gombrowicz as works of cultural denunciation, the denunciation of certain aspects of social life; in the second part I will situate this analysis within a larger sociological and cultural criticism which is implicit in this theater and relate it to the possibilities of going beyond such a problematic.

Before passing to these two elements of my essay, however, I would like to introduce briefly a few important problems that are clearly theoretical and abstract, but within which the entire problem of denunciation is located: namely, what is the artistic work in general and the theatrical work in particular? What are their relations to the human condition, to human and social reality?

I believe that the entire problematic of modern society and, within this society, the problematic of contemporary cultural creations lies in the fundamental relation between the real and the possible. In this regard, furthermore, Marxist thought has done nothing but carry on the tradition of classical philosophy. From Pascal to Lenin passing through Kant, Hegel and Marx, this tradition has always persisted in defining man, above all, according to a twofold dimension as a being who lives in a given world but, at the same time, capable of going beyond this world, of transforming it from within; and, taking it as his starting point, being capable of directing it elsewhere — toward something beyond him. Now, the relationship between the real and the possible is dialectical because they depend on each other. The possible is based on the real, but the possible only becomes real insofar as it is an overcoming and a modification of the real as it exists. On the other hand, existing reality is nothing but the realization of a previous possible reality.

One of the fundamental ideas of Pascal, Hegel, Marx, Lukacs and all those philosophers and thinkers in this line of thought is that one cannot define man as one does an object. An object exists, is worn down and transformed, but it does not transform itself. Man, on the other hand, is not only the object of transformations but also the subject of them. An alternation of the double dimension of the real and the possible is historically verified. When man's possibilities are accentuated, change, pushed to the utmost, tends to lead to the theory of man as an absolute creator, a theory in which obstacles, such as the real, the positive and the given, are forgotten. When, instead, man's possibilities are reduced, he is seen as an object, as a being defined by his adaptation to existing reality (theorists have described this as reification), thus reducing and even eliminating the possible.

Anticipating the conclusion of my exposition, I should add that the major problem of modern industrial societies in the West is (to an extent still unknown to our society) the danger of reduction or even elimination of the dimension of man's possibilities. To be convinced of this, one need think only about the works of Adorno and Marcuse and the rest of the Frankfurt School. These theorists denounce the risk of suppressing the possible and the risk of entrenchment in a simply positivistic world of the given, in which man will have his place but will have completely lost his desire to struggle and to go beyond the given. With respect to such a danger hidden in advanced industrial societies, one should always remember that culture in general and the work of art in particular are closely linked to the dimension of the possible. It is often stated that the work of art permits man to become aware of himself. I would push this even further by stating that it is, first of all, a phenomenon which allows man to become aware not only of what he is, but also of what he can become — his aspirations and possibilities. This is like saying that if in a given society the dimension of the possible is reduced, or even suffocated, then the possibility of the artistic, philosophical and cultural creation is profoundly menaced. We will return to this problem later.

With the question defined in this way, I would now like to try to define the structure of the work of art as well as its function and nature. Our work resumes and continues Kant's aesthetics, which defines the work according to two dimensions: unity and richness (and such a definition, moreover, not only refers to the work of art, but is also applicable to science and behavior). Therefore, the work of art is the result of a surmounted tension between two poles which are extreme richness (that is, to a large extent, the given, the existing world and the immediately perceived) and extreme unity (which is connected to action, transformation, in short, the possible). I would even say that undoubtedly too much emphasis in Marxist works has been placed on unity, at the expense of richness. (This includes our own works on the cultural creation and is one of the valid objections which we are now overcoming.)

The point is that if the artistic work is defined by its unity, that is, by its coherence, still this is not its only dimension, as we will see in the following concrete analysis. It goes without saying that unity also exists at the level of science. The external world, the bottle standing before me, is not a given. It was created by man who, with the help of concepts, organizes the given, creates the object at the level of perception and the principles of conservation or reversibility at the scientific level. In the field of the artistic work, however (and Kant said it very clearly), man does not create concepts, but rather a global universe which in turn is defined according to the two poles of unity and richness. Contrary to science, though, the work of art does not know concepts. Its universe is made of characters and individual situations, words, colors, sensible materials and sounds.

Since traditional criticism was, above all, dedicated to describing the richness of a work, all the works based on Marxist aesthetics were, until now, oriented toward what that criticism had neglected, that is, the investigation of unity, the bringing to light of the internal coherence of the work. Here, for example —

and I hope I am forgiven if I cite my own work — I might add my investigation of unity in the works of Pascal, Racine, Malraux or Genet. But there are perfectly coherent works that do not offer the least aesthetic interest because their subject is too poor to arouse even the slightest degree of tension between the two poles.

By way of answering the objection brought against Marxist aesthetics for not being in the least concerned with the richness of a work, my collaborators and I have thoroughly examined this problem, and I will give the partial conclusion of our study to you. Of course, it would be very difficult to make an inventory of such richness, so much the more so as methodological works on this point are very scarce. I will add, nevertheless, that there are at least three important fields that are a part of it — without being exhaustive.

To the extent that the unity of an artistic work is based on a significant world view, which is a way of conceiving life and of imagining a possible and rigorously valid life for the realization of values, the first difficulty that one must integrate is an ineluctable biological phenomenon: death.[1] A world view is a rule for living and acting, a solution to the problem of adaptation and of overcoming life's obstacles. Its significance is in permitting a group or an individual to adopt to a situation and, since thought and action are connected to each other, to make life possible in its environment. But this attempt to live collides incessantly with the problem of death. It follows that every work of art will pose the problem of death according to its richness and the given, but with nuances because some views (for example, rationalism) eliminate it while others (literature and existential philosophy) place it at the center of their universe.

Another field which is part of the richness of a work is the erotic, to which Freud has drawn our attention and certain aspects of which every world view and system of coherence forbid. Social life — and the work of art, culture, and history are part of community life — necessarily implies the repression of a sector of erotic life, but not always the same. And, to the very extent that the work is a synthesis of richness and unity, it is valid in as much as it integrates this richness with its unity and coherence, and in

---

1. I have based my reflections on Julia Kristeva's analyses of the work of M. Bakhtine, in *Critique*, No. 239 (1967).

as much as it also expresses the degree of validity in what is opposed to this unity which it sacrifices. Certainly, there is a danger in wanting to reduce the work of art to the erotic aspect alone — and more particularly, we will soon see this with respect to the psychoanalytic and psychological interpretations of Genet's writings — but this aspect, nevertheless, exists as an element of richness organized by the work's coherence, and which must be integrated. One of the characteristics of great works of art is that of expressing the sacrifice imposed by coherence.

Finally, there is also a social sector in the richness of a work of art. Perhaps it is here that the work — if it is valid — has a particularly critical function. Indeed, everything which in social life and thought is sacrificed by a certain type of unity is part of this richness. Unity does not express society in its totality. It is the world view of particular groups in society and, for this reason, is repressive in relation to the view of other groups. Thus, in Molière's *The Misanthrope* Jansenism is rejected. I have tried to show how such a condemnation is justified in the perspective of the group which he expresses (the nobility of the court). And yet, to understand this text it is very important to see the extent to which Molière also speaks about the human value of the absolute spirit and the limitation imposed on man by the defense of good sense with the refusal to integrate a character of the magnitude of Alceste.

Many other aspects of the richness of an artistic work exist, but I wanted only to point out that the two poles coexist in the work, that which assigns them both a critical and dogmatic function. Critical to the extent that it always expresses man's possibilities, as well as the values which he sacrifices to the unity of a world view; dogmatic to the extent that it always has before it — if it is valid — the reality of man. Without being either ideological or conceptual, it expresses at the artistic level of a universe of characters, colors and sounds what philosophy expresses with the concept and what is likewise the essence of action: the ordering of the given, the external world, through the thought, fantasy, and, above all, the action of man. It is connected to a world view, to the assertion of certain values and, thus, is part of the human condition and the necessity of any group whatsoever to accept a certain dogmatism, a certain unity in other words.

Let me specify what might seem rather theoretical in this introduction: we must avoid playing with words that often designate very different things from each other. It is not a question of dogmatism in the sense of being faithful to a past that one would like fixed and immutable, but of a dogmatism constituted by the limits imposed by any creation and any search for unity. When at the level of perception I say that this is a bottle, when at the level of science I assert the validity of the principle of conservation or reversability, we are dealing with a unity created by consciousness, with an ordering of data and, at most, with an entire global and integral universe which the activity and behavior of man tend to create. In every valid cultural creation and in every human life (and the more that this is so, the more valid it is), there is a synthesis of passivity and reception with activity and the organization of richness received from the world. This synthesis amounts to a unitary view. No human life, and thus no culture, is possible except within these two dimensions. To the extent that a society suppresses the activity of men and makes them passive, to that extent does it risk the harmonious development of the human personality. This is true even if society provides all the information available, by means of television and the mass media. In as much as the individual is unable to synthesize such information, he implicitly loses the effect of the cultural creation and his life will be limited to a process of passive adaptation. It is due to his education and formation that he cannot organize this information into a unity that is connected to action, thought and the cultural creation.

Therefore, it is within this problematic that the problem of contemporary art is posed and, more specifically, that of sociological and cultural denunciation which is the topic of my essay. It is within this problematic that I would like to analyze the theatrical works that brilliantly and rigorously raise the problem of the structure of our society and, consequently, man's relationship to it. This is done in a highly realistic way and sets realism against naturalistic documentation and immediate description. I am referring to the work of the Polish writer Witold Gombrowicz, who so far has given us two famous texts, *Yvonne* and *Le Mariage*, and above all to the work of Jean Genet, especially his last four works, *Les Bonnes*, *Le Balcon*, *Les Nègres* and *Les Paravents*. His first work, *Haute Surveillance*, offers less interest for my theme.

In both instances, of course, I will insist on what gives coherence, unity and meaning to these works, without thereby forgetting their richness which constitutes an essential element of their aesthetic value. As I have already said, however, I will not stress this latter aspect. Besides, those who have read the works or have seen them performed will remember them well enough.

Before beginning my analysis of these works, I would like to connect my method to a very important problem, the reception of the works themselves. Indeed, the way in which they are received by the public and the critic is indicative of specific mental structures within modern society. For example, when *Le Mariage* was performed in Paris, the critics unanimously considered it an oneiric and incoherent work. Instead, it was rigorously coherent and meaningful, as I will try to demonstrate. To the extent that critics have tried to find a meaning for at least part of the work, if not all of it, they were immediately and spontaneously drawn to the individual Gombrowicz and the Oedipus complex rather than to a world view (which is always collective). This came about because they relied upon one of the first scenes in which there are two youths just back from the war who find themselves in a milieu in which other characters appear both familiar and strange to them. The two young men are speaking a language which the others both know and do not know. Suddenly, they realize that they are in front of the paternal house of one of them, which is now an inn. They are also facing this youth's fiancée, who has become a prostitute, and his father, who is now the innkeeper. They realize that the language they are speaking is that of their childhood. Now, in considering this scene, no critic even for a moment has thought of the father's house as an evocation of the youth's country and the mother's language, his maternal tongue. All this seems evident as the work unfolds. After having read the "dossier" containing almost all of the articles written about the play, I assure you that no one in the least alluded to such an interpretation and that the only explanation given resorted to the Oedipus complex.

Another more recent example: someone told me that the Living Theater had used only male actors in performing *Les*

Bonnes, "as Genet wanted it." Surprised by this statement, I re-read the preface to the work, in which Genet explicitly states that the waiters must be impersonated by women and that the problem of their sex is of little importance. In fact, the matter is otherwise quite important, as we will soon see. But, just as the father and mother "are" the Oedipus complex for Gombrowicz, so, in order to find the meaning of Genet's work, critics immediately think of the homosexual aspect of his novels and life.

Actually, one can undeniably give an individualistic meaning to any human action and, implicitly, to any written text. The social level of organization can also drive elements of such an individualistic meaning into the unconscious. There is, however, a fundamental and total break between the coherence of a single subject and the coherence of the collective subject, the group. The former subject can be sacrificed and repressed by the social organization, since it is within the social and cultural realm. The latter tends to resolve its existential problems in a given environment and largely in a non-conscious way. Indeed, the French philosophical tradition from Descartes to Sartre has been too inclined toward a philosophy of consciousness in general and toward individual consciousness. Because of this, it has ignored a fundamental aspect of reality and has left no space to reflect on it. This aspect may be described in the following way: reason and sensation already exist at the biological level (a hungry cat which traps a mouse acts meaningfully, i.e., we can translate its actions into terms of problem and solution); on the other hand, at the human level, when consciousness appears (along with its corollaries, language and communication), it is undoubtedly an indispensible and inevitable element, but only an element of meaning not wholly conscious of collective behavior. And I will add that any valid work of art expresses the individual problems of the author but, at the same time, also the coherence of the collective view of which he is a part.

By examining human behavior and its expressions, I would say that at one end one finds behavior that, above all, expresses precisely individual realities. Freud has called this behavior "libidinal," where the interlocutor is always considered as an

---

2. Cf. "The Subject of the Cultural Creation," which appears in this volume.

object either of desire or repulsion. We have thousands of such expressions as the writings and designs of alienated and sick people. In these instances, however, one cannot include the work of art. If — as Freud has shown — alienation, dreams and madness are perfectly coherent with respect to the individual subject, one must add that a dream is not an art work precisely because its coherence disturbs social logic. At the other end, one finds works that express individual realities in such a way as to express social coherence at a very rigorous level, rather than disturb this coherence. This, for example, is the case with the works of Gombrowicz and Genet. Between these two extremes, madness and genius, there are numerous variations, and the mixing of individual and collective problems makes up the plot of our consciousness and our daily life.

The crucial thing in approaching a cultural creation, then, is to view the individual problems expressed there as an aspect of that richness which must be made coherent and which must be inserted into the social logic without disturbing it. That is why it seems to me rather questionable to reduce Genet's work to problems of personal exorcism, or Gombrowicz's to the Oedipus complex. It is eminently a social problem with which we are dealing, that of man's life in a degraded world.

The works of these two writers pose the problem of culture and values in a universe that is undoubtedly imaginary, but which is profoundly linked to current social life. First of all, I will try to show the global coherence of their works. Then, since our recent work has permitted us to extend this analysis to include stylistic elements, I will give some conclusions on the microstructures that we have discovered in the first 25 lines of Genet's *The Blacks* (*Les Nègres*).

I will begin by studying the theater of Gombrowicz because I would like to treat Genet's work more extensively. As far as I know, Gombrowicz has written only two theatrical works, *Yvonne* and *Le Mariage*. Both recreate an imaginary world linked to two historical moments of Polish society: in *Yvonne* an antebellum description of the ruling classes of that society; and in *Le Mariage* the new society that emerged from the war and the establishing of a popular democracy, especially the imaginative rendering of the events that generated it. I also immediately add that one finds a similar problematic for Western societies at the center of Genet's *Le Balcon*.

Yvonne is a rather simple drama in appearance. It is the story of a prince who rules over an imaginary realm and who falls in love with a common woman called Yvonne, princess of Bourgogne, whom he marries. This creates an enormous scandal at court, where many beautiful girls spend their time dreaming of becoming princess. The prince then tires of his caprice — in this he is backed by the entire court — and decides to kill Yvonne. After doing so, life goes on "normally." Written in 1935, the drama has come under attack often, but no one, as far as we know, has considered Yvonne's function in the imaginary realm. According to the perspective of Christian existentialism at the base of the entire work, its structure is linear and very specific. We have before us an encounter between the court (composed of the king, the queen, the prince and their courtesans) and the "essence" of life. The encounter is unbearable because this essence reveals the truth in a society in which everyone obstinately persists in hiding it from himself and others. Finally, this situation becomes so intolerable that it is unanimously decided to suppress it in order to re-establish the earlier situation. Yvonne stands for the presence of nothing, the absolute, the absence of quality, or of any concrete position within the world. (And yet, she says she believes in God.) She does not speak — throughout the play she has eight brief lines, but 27 stage directions indicate that she remains quiet — but her presence alone will cause all the truths hidden under the everyday lies of that realm to emerge.

The first to emerge are totally soothing. One learns that a certain noble lady has false teeth, another false breasts, and another a distorted foot. These are physical defects, of course, but when revealed they create a great deal of affliction and provoke animosity toward Yvonne. Later on, these truths that we gradually discover become more serious. The king is suddenly reminded of the assassination by which he has been able to take the throne, an assassination that he had removed from his heart. Yvonne's mere presence stirs up in him the desire to be himself and to continue killing. The queen fears that her most intimate secret has been snatched from her. In performing her role in society, she loves poetry and writes verses. As for the prince, who only wanted to marry Yvonne in order to scandalize the court and to break the monotony of daily life, he suddenly realizes that he is prevented from playing his princely role and from leading the life he carried on previously. In short, nothing in society can continue to function without the intruder, Yvonne, being removed. Individually and without conscious agreement, the protagonists find themselves in the same room and with the same plan: to kill her. Nothing remains but to study the most "correct" way to do it, to have it occur "from above" and to respect the rules. After some discussion, it is decided to have her swallow a fish whose bones will choke her. Once the assassination is carried out, there is another problem: what to do with the body. Since Yvonne is a princess, a period of national mourning is decreed involving all the signs of sorrow. With order re-established, the lies can exist once again. Even if the prince still has some scruples in delighting in the situation, since he retains a vague remembrance of his guilt in the deed, he too will finally forget it and will take up his usual life.

Yvonne has a relatively simple structure in that the different modes of inauthentic existence within a specific social group are made apparent through a confrontation with one and the same character. The structure of *Le Mariage,* on the other hand, is much more complex. Like Genet's *Le Balcon,* it adds the further dimension of time and becoming. For the sociologist, this poses the problem of finding out in what way such a problematic informs these works. Although received by critics as an absurd and purely oneiric work, it rigorously presents the poetic representation of the social transformations that occurred in the popular democracies of central Europe. The perspective is that of an aristocratic Polish emigrant. As I already said at the start of my essay, in the first scenes we see two boys, Henri and Jeannot, returning from the war and finding themselves in a strange environment and in the presence of strange people whom they knew long ago. The house of Henri's father has become an inn, his parents the innkeepers and his fiancée a prostitute. This is due to the threat of a drunkard, a man of the people, whom Henri's father fears. This threat degrades everything, even though the drunkard is also terrorized by the "immobile figure of the father" and does not dare attack him openly. As a result, we have fear and the sense of a threat reciprocally balancing each other.

Once the two youths grasp the situation, they ally themselves with the father and the balance is upset. When Henri kneels before his father, order and legitimacy are re-established. The father becomes king, the fiancée becomes a princess, and the drunkard is thrown into prison. Preparations are begun for a legitimate marriage.

Soon, however, the drunkard escapes and returns to the court while the marriage preparations are being made. Turning to Henri, he explains that he is also a priest, though not connected to a traditional religion such as Henri's ("high" religion) but to a "low" religion that is "humanly human, lowly, unofficial, obscure and blind, earthly and savage." He proposes an alliance so that they might establish another order of legitimacy, overthrow his father the king and so that he, Henri, might become king through his own decision. After some uncertainty, Henri accepts the drunkard's alliance and the balance is once again upset. Just as the father had become king through Henri's help, so the drunkard now becomes a very powerful ambassador with real historical power. Henri takes power but is not satisfied in locking up his father and other dignitaries. He also has the drunkard thrown into prison, whence he rules alone, as a true dictator. Before disappearing, however, this last "priest of a human, earthly and savage religion" marries Jeannot and Henri's fiancée.

As a result, Henri will not be able to re-establish an order of legitimacy. On the occasion of his marriage feast, he will demand that Jeannot kill himself. This is agreed upon and Henri is again in power by himself. He is not sure, however, whether he governs the policemen surrounding him or whether they are overseeing him. While Jeannot's corpse is being carried away, Henri explains his action in a monologue: "If I'm imprisoned here, down there, elsewhere and far away, may my act be raised to supreme heights! And may the funeral march lead there!"

One may see here a rigorous poetic description of the events that took place after World War II in central European countries, where the grave social crisis resulting from the conflict depended for its solution on the attitude of the combatants and intellectuals returning from the front. If this description takes on a nightmarish aspect, it is because the viewpoint is that of an aristocrat. Further, the events that took place ended with the suppression of the aristocracy, the death of its values and the suppression of history. By revolting, the people endanger the values which form the basis of the traditional social order. Still, they cannot overthrow this order by their efforts alone. This is brought about by the precarious balance of power between the father and the drunkard at the beginning of the drama.

Henri and Jeannot represent the combatants and intellectuals and their attitude will resolve the conflict. First, we see them side with traditional values, religion and legitimacy. The defense of religion and Christian values, however, is no longer a problem of morality for them. They easily allow themselves to be seduced by that new "human and earthly" religion that can re-establish a new order of legitimacy based on humanistic values. Now, a new and valid human order was not able to be brought about through such an alliance with the people, but rather the omnipotence of the executive and a dictatorship. Although there is a total victory of the oppressors and the governors — and we will find this echoed in *Le Balcon* — still, *Le Mariage* somewhat faintly conserves the echo of a continuing action. Henri hopes that his "act will be raised to supreme heights."

As for Jeannot's suicide, it seems to me that precisely because Gombrowicz write the play from an aristocratic perspective, he was able to see what someone else, more involved in the new society, could have discovered only with great difficulty: that Henri and Jeannot or, if you prefer, Stalin and Trotsky, the new rulers and those who remained in opposition, were not at first antagonists but brothers of one and the same character — the revolutionary intellectuals. Later, events made dictators out of some and opponents out of others. The first forgot their revolutionary ideals in taking power, the second still hope to establish a new order of legitimacy but are unable to fight back in their oppositional role. These "commit suicide" in order to guarantee the country's unity, faced as it is with the new threat of war.

Thus, in this play we have all the elements of the events that took place to culminate only in the omnipotence of the governors: a revolutionary situation which could have been resolved only by a return to traditional values. With the position which the intelligentsia took, however, the situation ended in a dictatorship. For Gombrowicz, who maintains that nothing can be done outside the religious realm and that of traditional values, man has become degenerate and has suppressed history. Line by line, situation by situation, the work is rigorously coherent. All the blindness of criticism is needed to have recognized only an incoherent dream or an expression of the Oedipus complex in the play.

If I have dealt at length with this work, it is because it seems to offer a good example of cultural denunciation in contemporary theater and because we will find the same denunciatory problematic in *Le Balcon*, only this time applied to the West.

As far as I know, the first characteristic of Genet's theater is that in contemporary avant-garde literature, it alone stages groups rather than individuals. In fact, all of his work, except for *Haute Surveillance*, which is still centered on the same problematic as his novels, sets groups, rather than individuals, against each other, waiters against lord and lady; revolutionaries against the people on the balcony (the bishop, the general, the judge, the queen and her servant); blacks against whites; and finally, in *Les Paravents*, the group formed by Saïd (Leila and Mother) against three successive orders of oppression, victorious revolt and the dead. We are quite far from the individualistic perspective of a certain type of criticism!

The second characteristic is that these four works have a common structure that is gradually enriched and transformed. I would like to cite a critique that shows very precisely where the public's misunderstanding of these works lies:

"Genet's theater states that appearance and ritual, as theater within a theater, has an ideal value in relation to the mediocrity of reality. But one then asks: Why do those who live through ritual kill themselves? If appearance represents value, it is impossible to understand either the waiters' suicide or Roger's self-mutilation in *Le Balcon*. Either Genet's plays are incoherent, and as a rather brilliant critic said, Genet is a genius at the beginning of his works, but at the end he proves to be poor; or the universe of his plays is completely different from what criticism thinks it sees in them."

The particularly important problem of the relations between the real and the imaginary is, in fact, connected and even subordinated to the central theme of the conflict between oppressed and oppressors. In this conflict the oppressed carry out a ritual both of hate and fascination, in which they destroy the oppressors and identify with them. In *Les Bonnes*, Claire and Solange pretend to be Madame and then pretend to kill her. In *Le Balcon* the ritual is performed by two related groups of the oppressed: the small fry who go to the house of illusions where they identify with the mighty on the balcony, and the rebels who kill these very same people. In *Les Nègres*, the oppressed ritually assassinate a white woman but cannot help being fascinated by her. Finally, in *Les Paravents* we find similar elements, although not as notable because the ritual is part of a partially changed vision that includes the real victory of the rebels.

In the conflict between the two groups, the oppressed represent values. The oppressors are only inauthentic and hateful caricatures, such as Madame or the white dignitaries in *Les Nègres*. Unlike the oppressed, however, they have something that is authentic, real and fascinating: power. The oppressed, who only experience values authentically in the imaginary realm of ritual, cannot really kill Madame or overthrow the mighty on the balcony. Still, already in *Les Nègres*, but especially in *Les Paravents,* the situation is changed and hope for victory appears for the first time, followed by the actual victory of the oppressed.

Undoubtedly, the ritual of hate and fascination exists as the only authentic value in the universe of these works, but this is insufficient to the extent that what is demanded in reality cannot be won. The oppressed are too weak to struggle against the powerful marionettes who dominate them. For this reason, they can only destroy themselves: thus, Claire's suicide and Solange's condemnation and Roger's self-mutilation. Since authentic reality is inaccessible, physical death can honor only the placing of values in that essential death which is the imaginary. In these four works by Genet, the values of the imaginary realm intrude upon the real world, thereby reinforcing the hope of the oppressed. If it is impossible to overcome Monsieur and Madame in *Les Bonnes*, if the revolt is suppressed in advance in *Le Balcon*, in *Les Nègres* a victorious revolt is possible. Finally, in *Les*

Paravents the revolt is victorious, although it still proves insufficient.

Beginning with *Les Bonnes*, two particularly significant scenes illustrate the structure of this universe and what is authentic in the imaginary realm of ritual in relation to the act of deriding the real. The waiters have falsely denounced Monsieur, who is then imprisoned. In performing their ritual in which they identify with Madame, however, they express real love for Monsieur. They declare that they will follow him all the way to prison and will do everything to mitigate his punishment. Then Madame arrives and says exactly the same thing, only with some stylistic variations that make her speech particularly ridiculous and hateful. First, convinced that Monsieur will not be condemned, she decides to follow him, but in a conditional way. Then she turns to Solange, showing by this that she is speaking only to the audience.

As the work unfolds, we see that the waiters, unfortunately, will not be able to attain an authentic reality. Monsieur is freed. It becomes evident that they will be condemned for false testimony and will not even be able to continue their daily ritual. A final attempt to kill Madame proves to be as vain as previous ones. Only one way remains for them to escape: death. Claire, who plays Madame, will oblige Solange solemnly to offer her the poison in a precious cup, from which she will drink. Meanwhile, facing the audience, he will remain still, with his hands crossed as if they were handcuffed. Before dying, Claire will say to him: "We'll go all the way. I will assume our two existences. You'll have to be very strong. . . . And when I'm condemned, don't forget to carry me inside you. Preciously. We'll be beautiful, free and happy. Solange, we don't have a minute to lose. . . ."

When Solange is condemned, he is no longer just a waiter but "Miss Solange Lemercier. . . Madame's equal, who walks with her head held high." Madame's destruction can be carried out only on the imaginary level. Theirs is a moral victory, though, since they have pushed themselves to the extreme in order to realize the values of the imaginary level. Actually, they live according to appearances, while Madame — a ridiculous liar — lives a real life in appearance only. This was so from the beginning and nothing can be changed. Madame cannot be conquered. In order to preserve the seriousness and authenticity of their existence, the waiters were forced to destroy themselves, even if this self-destruction has become an apotheosis.

In *Le Balcon*, the structure of the conflict is similar, but more complex. As in Gombrowicz's *Le Mariage*, Genet has introduced a historical element: the conflict between oppressed and oppressors, but also a collective awareness of the omnipotence of the executive powers and a poetic representation of the events that have led to such an awareness.

The poor, who enter the house of illusions in order to take on the roles of the bishop, the judge and the general, find out that the essence of these three dignitaries can exist only imaginatively. The actual bishop cannot incarnate the essence of the priesthood since he is always forced to make compromises in order to perform his function. Moreover, the poor think that they are identifying with the mighty, traditionally represented by the church, the magistracy and the army, while in reality, society has changed. The owner of the house of illusions holds the real power, that is, Madame Irma and her associate, the chief of police.

Outside, two groups begin the revolt. One is guided by Chantal, a girl belonging to the house of illusions who now joins in the revolt. She becomes the muse of the insurgents insofar as she incarnates the values of anarchy and humanism. The other group is led by Roger, who is in love with Chantal but knows that in order to bring about the revolution one must temporarily set those values aside and form a disciplined and hierarchical organization. The rebels succeed in killing the real bishop, judge and general, and they shatter the queen's prestige, perhaps even subduing her. But in the house of illusions, Madame Irma and the chief of police organize the forces of resistance. Society always needs a bishop, a judge and a general. Therefore, they suggest to the poor people that in their ritual they play the role of those three dignitaries in order to replace them in reality. By accepting such dignified roles, moreover, they lose the value they had in the imaginary realm. Instead, they become ridiculous puppets. Madame Irma, then, substitutes for the queen.

The revolt, however, is defeated. Chantal is killed and she is remembered by the new power holders. Roger finds himself alone. At the end, he realizes that the governing powers alone are in control. He enters the house of illusions and asks if he can play the part of the chief of police. This is what Irma and the real police chief expected for some time, and the slave sings about his glory. Roger is quick to realize, however, that ritual is not enough, since it embodies no real power. Unable to sustain this state of affairs, he mutilates himself — another formula for indicating his submission. The chief of police can then enter the mausoleum awaiting him and from there he will rule the consciousness of society for 2,000 years.

See how this work rigorously represents the historical events of Western society? The social and political crisis that followed the end of World War II had created a revolutionary situation. Contrary to what has occurred in the U.S.S.R. and then in central Europe, though, the revolutionary forces were defeated. Notwithstanding this, the two lines of historical evolution both ended in a similar way: governmental domination through revolutionary victory in the U.S.S.R. and the popular democracies, and through its defeat in western Europe. It is worth noting the extent to which the poetic representation of such events gives coherence to the universe of these two plays by Gombrowicz and Genet.

With *Les Nègres*, we take a step forward in the problematic of the conflict between oppressed and oppressors. Here, ritual presents a unique aspect. Contrary to what we have seen in *Les Bonnes* and *Le Balcon*, ritual does not counterbalance reality on the stage. This one finds only behind the scenes. It is Ville de Saint-Nazaire who periodically connects what occurs on stage with the action taking place outside. All of the characters belong to the oppressed and are black. Periodically, they ritually assassinate a white woman. Outside, for the moment, the blacks have succeeded only in killing one of their own who, it seems, had betrayed them.

The scheme is thus far rather similar to the one we have seen in the first two works. A new element is added when Ville de Saint-Nazaire announces that another leader had entered into the streets, one who perhaps will lead the blacks to victory. It is with a note of hope, then, that the drama ends.

Besides this profound change in the problematic, there is also an aesthetic problem within the global structure, the resolution of which has brought about important changes at the level of the action itself. Since the ritual concerns the radical opposition between blacks and whites (the killing of the latter and the breaking off of contacts between the two groups), it was then impossible to have white actors play the roles of the white characters. Indeed, a production based on hate for whites and their destruction would have intrinsic contradictions to the extent that the two races collaborated in the play's realization.

As a result, if whites are needed on stage, as Genet says in his preface, black actors must also impersonate the whites. Even more, the audience must understand this impersonation. That is why at a certain point in the work the black actors take off their white masks in order to present themselves along with the others who participate in the ritual killing of the whites. The white characters whom we see on the balcony (the missionary, the judge, the governor, the queen and the valet — who, moreover, also appear in the previous work, thus revealing the link uniting the two texts) are at a level that is half-hidden, half visible, although present in the work when the oppressed perform their ritual. Contrary to what took place in *Les Bonnes* or *Le Balcon*, where Monsieur and Madame on the one hand, and Madame Irma, the chief of police and the other dignitaries on the other, represented the real as opposed to the imaginary, in *Les Nègres* reality is placed offstage.

With the glimpse of hope occasioned by the arrival of the new leader who perhaps will lead the blacks to victory, the meaning and action of the ritual will take on a completely new sense. While at first the oppressed were doomed to defeat and condemnation, now we will see them destroy the whites. The real hope of victory is expressed by the two lovers, Village and Virtue, in the final lines. They do not want to join in the ritual, since they want to spend their time in loving each other. They are brought back by Archibald, who is in charge of the game and who explains to them that in the world of the oppressed love can only be expressed by words taken from the oppressors. When the ritual is over, Village and Virtue see a chance to discover new words, "black" words, which will allow them to express their love authentically and in a world of their own.

The integral structure of the work also covers its partial structures; these we have called "microstructures." The two criticisms brought against the Marxist analysis of literature are that it is concerned only with the global structures of a work, its coherence and unity, and that it neglects its richness and form in the strict sense, that is, its style. When studying *Les Nègres* with a group of young scholars from the Centre de Sociologie of the Université Libre in Brussels, I wanted to control the global analysis in a rigorous way. With this aim, we began to study the play line by line. At the specifically semantic level, we already discovered a complex network of microstructures in the first 25 lines. Each sentence is justified in relation to the one preceding or following it, but is also related to the global structure.

In the short time remaining, it is difficult to sum up our conclusions, since they are incomplete and must be taken up again next year. These first 25 lines constitute a reduced model of the entire work and there are two other smaller models within the reduced one. I must add, furthermore, that we were able to find these models almost without seeking them because we are undoubtedly faced with a simple example of the structural relation between the work and its elements. There are probably other, more complex relations, but we have not gone far enough to be able to discover them.

The first reduced model is given in the first two lines. We find Archibald, who is in charge of the *jeu*, presenting the blacks of the ritual to the audience and to the court (of whites). As they are presented, they salute the audience. He announces their names one by one, giving them pompous and clearly borrowed "white" names. He also describes their makeup: "Just as you have lilies and roses, so we — in order to serve you — use our beautiful shiny-black makeup," a smoky black color dipped in saliva. Then he announces the beginning of the show: "We embellish ourselves to please you. You are white and spectators. This evening we shall perform for you." The second line is the queen's, who, in addressing the missionary, declaims: "Bishop! Bishop-*in partibus!*" In these two lines there is the beginning of the solemn ceremony, the ritual in which the blacks take up the white man's language, the language of ceremony, although they assume their own condition (a smoke-black color). As for the queen, she speaks

Latin, the language whites use for ceremonial purposes, just as
the blacks spoke "white." The content of her line and the order of
her enunciation, however, correspond to the action of the play.
"Bishop! Bishop-*in partibus!*" implies the opposition "effective
power-nominal power, emptied of its content." These two lines,
then, constitute a reduced model: black aggression corresponds
to the white's loss of power.

Similarly, there is another group of lines that is apparently
unconnected either with what precedes or follows it. The valet
and the missionary suddenly realize that their chairs have disappeared. At the end of the play we will learn that the blacks
took them in order to put together a catafalque for the
assassinated white woman. If it is true that we do not realize this
at first, it is enough to see where these lines occur to realize that
Genet clearly points this out. The lines follow the queen's first
question, "Are they going to kill her?" (the white woman) and
they precede the missionary's reply, "But she's dead, Madame."
Here, then, the disappearance of the chairs is connected with the
assassination of the white woman in a reduced model, just as the
latter is connected to the global structure of the work.

Another line of Archibald's gives us the exact problematic of
the work: "If we cut our links, may a continent go adrift, and
may Africa sink or fly away...." The victory is possible but not
certain. The reduced model closes on the statement that the
names that Archibald has given to the oppressed are false.
Likewise, the play closes with the awareness that the words
borrowed from the whites are false and with the hope that Village
will succeed in finding real words, "black" ones, to express his
love for Virtue.

Due to the lack of time, I cannot linger over these microstructures any longer. I wanted only to demonstrate, at least in
this play, that the unity that organizes the work's richness at the
semantic level also resonates in its style. Of course, one needs to
do a great deal of concrete research to discover if such microstructures can also be applied to other works as well, or if they are
only present in works having exceptional coherence. We have
taken only an initial step in this direction, but perhaps one can
eventually arrive at a scientific theory of style that would permit
one to analyze an entire work according to a scheme that

addresses both its unity and its richness as these are related to the world view of a specific group.

Unfortunately, I see there is not time remaining for me to analyze *Les Paravents,* but I would not like to conclude before briefly posing the fundamental problem of the cultural situation in our present society. Indeed, capitalist societies are now passing through a historical phase that sociologists describe in various ways: consumer society, organization capitalism, mass society, etc., each of these designating one aspect of the social and economic transformations that took place in Western society after World War II. These transformations have had, and still have, many repercussions on the psychological structure of individuals and groups. You know what took place on the economic level. After the critical period of capitalism, in which the regulatory mechanisms of the free market had disappeared and were substituted by the development of monopolies and trusts, a new equilibrium came to light: that of self-regulatory mechanisms and, above all, governmental intervention and planning. Today, the latter has nearly consolidated its position.

Between the two wars, two crises quickly followed each other: the social and political crisis of the years 1917 to 1921 and the economic crisis of 1929-33, during which Hitler came to power (not to mention the events outside the industrialized countries, Spain and Italy). Parallel to this critical period of capitalism, a new world view gradually developed at the cultural, philosophical and literary levels: existentialism, which undoubtedly had its center in France with such works as Sartre's *Being and Nothingness* and *Nausea* and Camus' *The Stranger.*

Today, if governmental intervention, planning and the self-regulatory mechanisms of society are in the process of limiting internal crises, they still present another problem: that of the increasing division between a small social group of "technocrats" (those in all sectors of society who make the basic decisions) and a growing number of specialists (whose material existence is steadily improving and becoming more secure, thanks to the general improvement in the quality of life). The competence of the latter group continues to grow because its members are indispensable for the proper functioning of society. They are, however, reduced simply to carrying out decisions made elsewhere. This is as if to say that everything that is basic to the dimension of the possible in men's psychic structure — therefore also basic to the cultural creation — is suppressed. Activity disappears only to leave room for man's passivity and receptivity. The dimension of the possible, including those of action, responsibility and the cultural creation, are called into question. This occurs not through force or violence but through a very subtle process of integration in which rebellious efforts have an increasingly difficult time making themselves heard.

This is the immense risk presented by the society in which we live. If it continues to develop along these lines, we will reach the paradoxical situation of a society in which men, reduced to the state of pure consumption, will become "illiterate specialists." In other words, they will be competent in their areas, but completely passive and uninterested in all the other sectors of social life.

This means that the problematic of the cultural creation is completely different from what it once was. For example, let us take Marx's analyses developed in the 19th century. He rightly points out that the proletariat would inevitably move toward socialism since it could not have continued to bear its increasing misery. In industrial societies today, however, misery is almost non-existent (I am perfectly aware that this is not so for Third World countries), and socialism has not taken root. On the contrary, with the disappearance of misery, resistance to social conditioning has diminished and this conditioning process exercises an ever greater pressure on the individual at many different levels. The existence of a level of life increasingly based on the possibilities of consumption facilitates man's psychological adaptation to a society in which he increasingly behaves as a passive and irresponsible performer.

For this reason, we might ask if there is any possibility of reacting against this situation, if there is any possibility of changing the direction of things, of defending man's liberty and the hope for a society in which one's authentic self-realization will be guaranteed. There is a precise reply: a unified effort must be carried out simultaneously at the social and economic levels of reality and at the level of consciousness.

Indeed, an action at the social and economic levels alone can always be outflanked by the psychological and intellectual control that society has over its members. As we know, this frequently occurs in most Western countries where the dominant classes succeed in manipulating the discontent of the workers and their cadres (I am referring to the analyses of Herbert Marcuse, S. Mallet and A. Gorz), preventing the people from becoming aware of the fact that such discontent exists not only at the level of consumption and salary. It also exists at a more general level where the structure of the human being is ill-adapted to social reality, one which prevents him from developing and from expressing himself. This is so true that, in the end, conflict is always resolved and individuals appeased by a higher salary and an improvement of their material conditions.

Inversely, a purely cultural action is in turn doomed in advance if it cannot base itself on reality, or at least on a social and economic action that would allow men to conserve and develop those psychological structures that favor the comprehension of their condition. Thus, we are now passing through a crucial moment for the cultural life of the West. As I have always said, a writer represents only the world view of the group to which he belongs, and this view can in turn be elaborated only on the basis of the society in which the group itself lives. If the structure of this society eliminates creative and responsible activity, the dimension of the possible, it will become very difficult for the creative person to produce an imaginary universe that is both rich and coherent.

8. *Genetic Structuralism and Stylistic Analysis*

I

For years I have studied literature with the help of a method that I have called genetic structuralism. Until now, however, I have never tried to apply it to poetry.

This limitation has often been criticized, but I have always acknowledged it by pointing out that the investigation of an area so different from the one in which I have worked for years requires considerable effort. For external reasons, I was never able to carry out such an investigation. That is why, until proof to the contrary, I have preferred to leave open the problem of knowing if the genetic structuralist method could be used in analyzing modern poetry.

I also pointed out, though, that even granting this possibility, two things seemed likely:

(a) As in the study of prose works (and social facts in general), here, too, one would first have to isolate a significant *global* structure on which partial or more strictly formal structures are founded, and *on the basis of which* one should study them;

(b) With respect to poetry, non-semantic structures (syntactic, phonetic, associative, etc.) are perhaps particularly important and decisive.[1]

This said, I took up for the first time the study of a number of poetic texts. To my great surprise, the use of the genetic structuralist method immediately proved more fruitful than I had dared to hope.

To illustrate the possibilities of the genetic structuralist method in this area, I will present here a *provisory* analysis of a poem by Saint-John Perse.

---

1. I would add that, given my lack of competence in this domain, it was more difficult for me to study poetry.

I say provisory because the fundamental principle of my method is that one must not begin with details but with the comprehensive and integral model of a work. In this case, the text's unity is most likely made up of all the poems of the book or many books. It seems, though, that there is a technical difference between studying a unit of poetic texts and a play or a novel. Even if the collection of poems proves to be the essential and significant unifying factor, nevertheless it is obvious that each poem, in turn, is much more independent in relation to the whole than is a chapter of a novel or a scene from a tragedy.

Given the added difficulties in analyzing poetic texts, it seems possible and useful to investigate semantic models poem by poem before approaching the comprehensive model of the collection. It seems that one would have difficulty applying such a method to other literary genres.

Lacking collaborators specializing in linguistics, I would also like to point out that the analysis I will present is obviously partial and only constitutes the beginning of an investigation. Still, it appears quite interesting and I hope it will be able to initiate a fruitful discussion.

Before passing to the analysis itself, I would like to establish a few methodological points. Genetic structuralism, as I have used it so far, presupposes:

(1) The bringing to light of a work's *global* semantic model, the formation of which constitutes *the schema of a global system* of relationships between men and between them and the universe;

(2) The sociological study of the genesis of this model within the dynamic tendency of the collective consciousness of particular social groups;

(3) The extension of this global semantic structure into an aggregation of partial and more strictly formal structures, on all levels which the study of a written text involves.

Obviously, in the work that follows, we are not concerned with the second point. The sociological investigation could only concern the writer's total work and would require many years of study. For reasons indicated, we are also not going to exhaust the third point. What I propose to do here is only to delineate the comprehensive semantic model of *a* poem by Saint-John Perse and a *few* partial, semantic and syntactic structures.

Here, first of all, is the text:

> The rhythms of pride descend the red mornes.
> Turtles roll along the straits like brown stars.
> The roadstead forms a dream full of children's heads...
> Be a man, a calm-eyed man who laughs,
> a silent man who laughs under the calm wing of his eyebrow,
> perfect flight
> (and from the motionless border of the eyelash he goes back to
> things which he has seen,
> borrowing the paths of the fraudulent sea... and the motionless
> border of the eyelash
> he has made us more than one promise of isles,
> like he who says to one who is younger: "You will come!"
> And it's he who is in agreement with the captain of the ship).[2]

The Global Model

The universe of the poem seems to be built around the idea that cosmic and human values reside in an externally "motionless" spatial structure containing and permitting real *movement*. It is this synthesis between the static and the dynamic which alone assures one's mastery of the past and the future.

This idea can be found both in the text as a whole and in its individual elements. The first three sentences join together the terms suggesting movement to those suggesting stagnation: "rhythms" and "mornes" (hills like those in the Antilles); "roll along" and "straits"; "forms a dream" and "roadstead." Then we come to the image of man: "Be a man" is both an autonomous

---

2. Saint-John Perse, *Eloges*, Poème III (Gallimard, poetry collection), p. 30. The English translation is mine; the reader can refer to the original text below:

> Les rythmes de l'orgueil descendent les mornes rouges.
> Les tortues roulent aux détroits comme des astres bruns.
> Des rades font un songe plein de têtes d'enfants...
> Sois un homme aux yeux calmes qui rit,
> silencieux qui rit sous l'aile calme du sourcil, perfection du vol
> (et du bord immobile du cil il faut retour aux choses qu'il a vues,
> empruntant les chemins de la mer frauduleuse... et du bord
> immobile du cil
> il nous a fait plus d'une promesse d'îles,
> comme celui qui dit à un plus jeune: "Tu verras!"
> Et c'est lui qui s'entend avec le maître du navire).

Translator's note

norm and part of the sentence linked to the following qualifier. To "be a man," one must be a "calm-eyed man who laughs," a "silent man who laughs under the calm wing of his eyebrow." This represents perfection in the poem.

The word "wing" has already prepared us for the image of "flight." Both suggest a soaring bird whose body remains motionless while going forward. Added to these spatial descriptions are *time, action* and *values.* The motionless figure who laughs, and therefore who moves without moving, like the soaring bird, returns in his dynamic immobility to past things. He advances toward the "fraudulent" sea (in appearance stagnant but rich with "paths"). This permits him to "promise" "isles" (a suggestion of bliss), to awaken in the young hope in the future and to be in agreement with the one who controls the ship. Saint-John Perse is not more specific, but we may add that *in the poem* the function of the "captain of the ship" is homologous to that of the leader, God or humanity in the various philosophies of history. The poem, however, is not a philosophical text and, of course, in the poem "the captain of the ship" is not a leader, Gold or the collectivity, but simply the "captain of the ship."

Microstructures

Passing now to partial and formal structures in the strict sense of the word, I have been able to isolate a few with my very limited competence:

(a) The general form of the poem is made up of two static elements: the three syntactic or semantic lines at the beginning and the end of the poem that suggest a sort of symmetrical, static and regular container. These lines frame a much broader and livelier element of the text (separated, moreover, by a parenthesis to which I will return). This formal structure is, of course, homologous to the *global* (comprehensive) semantic structure (immobility containing movement, making the latter possible and valid although always subordinate to motionless space).

(b) These two groups of three propositions at the beginning and at the end of the poem, then, make up the poem's static element. Within each of these groups, however, there is a movement and a progression. In the first, spatial movement is respectively a *descent,* a *horizontal* advance and a flight into the imaginary. As for the last, the *orientation toward height* is not explicit but is only *suggested* by the word "heads."

The last three propositions have a symmetrical progression on the temporal level. The first unites the past tense of the verb to a future hope. The third implicitly suggests all three time dimensions in the "agreement with the captain of the ship."

(c) Along with the temporal progression in these last propositions, there is a corresponding diminution of externalization, from the *multiple* promises, a single assertion, to silence, the unspoken, the "agreement with the captain of the ship."

(d) In the first three propositions, the partial structures join the static and the dynamic respectively: "red mornes" (according to the dictionary, "morne" means height, hill. This semantically justifies its use, but for the reader who would most likely not think of this meaning, the word above all suggests the idea of a lack of variation and movement, opposed to the vivacity of color); "turtles roll along" (the turtle, a static animal, is opposed to "roll along"); "brown stars" (stars are usually bright).

(e) In the central part of the poem, the passage from "eyebrow" to "eyelash" provokes the spatial contraction of the word eyebrow (of which the eyelash is a part), to which corresponds a semantic progression (it is much more difficult for one to keep his eyelashes still than his eyebrows). Likewise, the paths of the fraudulent sea are statically framed by the *repetition* of "from the motionless border of the eyelash." Thus, we have a model which is both reduced and strengthened by the total poem.

(f) Finally, the parenthesis is a crucial part of the meaning of the poem's overall structure. Contrary to syntactic usage, the parenthesis is used here to introduce a break. It does not isolate a fragment within a text but breaks the poem in two, separating the first half which has a *spatial* character from the second half, which has a *spatio-temporal* character.

The parenthesis is an important but nevertheless secondary element with respect to the rest of the sentence. Therefore, this break expresses simultaneously the primary and dominant character of spatial immobility with respect to temporal progression and the control of the ship.

Undoubtedly, with this, the analysis of the poem is far from being complete and perhaps contains linguistic structures which still need to be brought to light. I only wanted to show what could be obtained by seeking *significant structures,* even in contemporary poetry.

I would like to conclude by asserting my conviction that this analysis, even incomplete, is a valid starting point for the study of a poetic text. *What is lacking* would follow upon what has already been done or upon another and better analysis, but one of the same type.

Finally, it goes without saying that the poem itself is only a partial structure within the global structure of the collection and eventually must be integrated into the latter. What I have isolated is not *the* meaning of *the* poetry of Saint-John Perse or a given number of its general characteristics. I have only analyzed a partial text which belongs to this global meaning and which is only *an element of it and nothing more.*

I would have liked to present to you still another related analysis of the first 27 lines of Jean Genet's *Les Nègres,* which also contains four reduced models of the play's global structure. Unfortunately, time does not permit me to do so.

Not being a linguist, I am very happy to have the occasion offered to me to here to present this analysis, because I do not know to what extent I have dealt with a general fact or only with two analyses of particular cases. In addition, the reduced model itself may be only a special case (the easiest to disclose) of an important phenomenon: the existence of microstructures functionally linked to the global structure of the work. Finally, my lack of competence and that of my collaborators has led us to limit our analyses to the semantic level, whereas similar structures may also exist on such other levels as the syntactic, phonological and rhythmical. There even may be structures that interfere on several different levels.

In my study on Racine (*The Hidden God*), I have already shown the extent to which one of the most famous lines of *Phèdre* ("The daughter of Minos and Pasiphaë") offers several reduced models of the play's global structure, both on the semantic and the phonetic levels. In spite of the limited time, I will mention an example that probably concerns a reduced model situated on two different levels. It was at the colloquium in Baltimore where Nicolas Ruwet criticized the different linguistic analyses of another line from *Phèdre*: "The sky is no more pure than the bottom of my heart." While he was developing his critique, I wondered if one could not find in this line a microstructural repetition of the play's global scheme: the union of opposites. In taking up the semantic meaning of the different elements, I obtained the following sequence: "The sky," which constitutes the summit of purity and value in the play (the heavens, the sun, purity); an element of negation, "is not," which leads us to its opposite; "more pure," which leads us back again to the same level as the sky; "the bottom," which once again leads us to the extreme opposite; and finally, "heart," to which I could not give any semantic value in situating it in relation to purity or impurity. It is when faced with this difficulty that I heard Ruwet say that "heart" needs to be compared to "pure" for phonological reasons — reasons that I had ignored and which I no longer clearly remember. When situated on two different levels, the reduced model was perfected. This is probably why this line has always been considered less beautiful than "the daughter of Minos and Pasiphaë," which contains one or more reduced models at each level.

Thus the analysis of microstructures leads us to what the classical definitions of the work of art have in common, from Kant and Hegel to Marx and Lukacs. As great as the differences may be between the ahistorical position of Kant, the historical idealism of Hegel and the historical materialism of Marx and Lukacs, they have one idea in common: the conception of the work of art as tension overcome, a tension on the non-conceptual level between an extreme richness and an extreme unity.

In all of my work I have tried concretely to describe this unity as the significant global structure of the different works that I have analyzed. With the discovery of microstructures, I can extend the concept of unity to style and to the order of propositions and words. If this hypothesis proves valid, there would then be a sociological level where the mental structures that constitute a world view may be elaborated. This world view is the global structure of the work and includes the stylistic level.

For the moment we have only the start of an investigation and a few hypotheses that I have been delighted to present here in order to submit them to your criticism and eventually to open up discussion.

II

When, as is the case here, a sociologist enters into discussion with the most distinguished representatives of another human science, there are two rules to follow: the first is to be extremely prudent in order to avoid misunderstandings; the second is to place the discussion only on those levels where it will be fruitful, i.e., the study of specific and precisely defined concrete facts. One might also discuss methodology and the general principles of research in the human sciences, which, to some extent, are common to the two disciplines.

For the moment, I would only like to raise three questions concerning general problems that are related to the talks that we have just heard.

I have listened to Mr. Benveniste's talk with a great deal of interest, especially the part where he insisted on the fact that some groups adopt the general language of society by adding their own perspectives and ideologies. This said, I would nevertheless like to formulate an objection and pose a question.

In effect, if I have understood correctly, Mr. Benveniste has told us that it is language that contains society and not the reverse. He based this assertion on the fact that one can study language apart from society but not society apart from language. It is precisely the contrary. In a relatively valid way, one can always study a part without studying the whole. . . but one cannot study the whole in leaving aside the parts. To take an example from literature, I can always study a scene from a play by Racine without studying the whole play. It is impossible, though, to study *Phèdre* or *Andromaque* without necessarily studying the scenes that form it. Thus, it is precisely because one can study language apart from society, and not the reverse, that one can argue that language is a part of social life rather than the latter being a part of language.

Moreover, I agree with Mr. Benveniste that one can find numerous aspects of language which reflect, express and explain given elements of social life and that language is a particularly important instrument for understanding social behavior. It is on this point, though, that I would like to raise a question which, despite appearances, is more than a mere terminological problem. Indeed, Mr. Benveniste has used such expressions as "language produces," "language interprets," "language governs" and "language creates." Usually, such an observation would reveal too much attention to details rather than a close examination of relatively comprehensive expressions. Given the contemporary intellectual context and especially this congress of linguistics, however, these expressions pose a particularly important theoretical problem.

Structuralism based on linguistics is currently a powerful theoretical movement in the human sciences. Taking structuralist linguistics as its paradigm, it ends up denying man's creative role and transfers the creativity factor to structures alone. One of the crucial discussions in the human sciences today is that of ascertaining whether it is men or structures that bring about historical transformations. Contrary to linguistically based structuralism, genetic structuralism asserts that in no instance could structures replace man as historical subject, even if they do characterize human thought, behavior and emotions. For example, Greimas writes, "Structures produce historical events." Todorov tells us that "men do not create language but language creates men." Althusser attributes the same creative role to social structures and the relations of production, forgetting that they are the result of men's actions and behavior.

That is why I would be grateful to Mr. Benveniste if he would specify what he means by these expressions. If it is only a question of approximations used to emphasize the importance of structures in comprehending human behavior, then I have no objection. Nor do I object if he wishes only to point out that men can do nothing outside of a structured language (I would add, a structured thought, structured social relations and structured emotions). If, however, one must take these expressions literally, they seem to me questionable because I do not believe that language produces, interprets, governs or creates. It is men who do so, through language and by using it as a privileged instrument, as Mr. Benveniste has clearly told us.

Finally, I would like to pose a question on method to Mr. Jakobson. Not being a linguist, however, I will proceed cautiously. Since I do not know the facts, I am ready to accept them as they have been presented. Mr. Jakobson has told us that in certain societies music and dance are inseparable. He spoke about a system of dance and music in which the two elements are always joined. But isn't there a preliminary methodological decision in this analysis by which dance is one structure and system of signs, music another and the expressions of these two systems are always joined? It seems just as likely that neither dance nor music are autonomous systems but only aspects or elements of a more comprehensive system. Only later are they differentiated. This, however, is an alternative that can be proposed only after an empirical investigation but, due to discussions I have had with other sociologists, I am especially sensitive to the danger of methodological presuppositions.

III

Listening to today's talks and discussions, I was surprised to learn that the major philosophical problems are still important for current scientific reflection. In this case I was thinking about the opposition between what such philosophies as those of Descartes, Kant or Husserl have in common (obviously, there are also very great differences among them) and the dialectical position of Hegel or Marx.

I will begin by briefly recalling the problem that Mr. Sebeok has raised. He has shown us how difficult it is to learn if one has the right to use the word "lie" in speaking about the language of animals and, from the outside, how difficult it is to say when an animal is actually in the process of "lying." Of course, you know that the problem is also relevant with respect to children and one must not confuse lying with storytelling.

There is also another closely related problem concerning the basis of the distinction between the immediate consumption of objects from the environment and the production of objects for consumption (or at the much more complex level of the production of the means of production). I think that it is much easier to find an answer to these two problems if one realizes that both are aspects of the fundamental distinction between the individual subject and the collective or transindividual subject. Obviously, animal behavior is individualistic, even in temporary or lasting animal societies, and could not imply a reflective or self-conscious dimension. That is why an animal cannot "lie" in the proper sense of the term, since lying presumes the distinction between it and the truth.

As for the child, the problem is related but not identical. It is in the process of socialization and will develop a reflective consciousness and an idea of the truth. Although the human being continues to behave in an individualistic way, even when an adult (dreams, slips, alienation), such behavior is much more characteristic of the child. It is this that is at the base of story-telling, which is not to be confused with lying. That which characterizes human beings and human societies and distinguishes them from animals and animal societies is the existence of the division of labor. This latter is also sophisticated and flexible enough to lead us to suppose the existence of a collective or trans-individual subject and reflective and theoretical consciousness. At this level one can easily define a lie and distinguish it from the libidinous forms of consciousness (dreams, slips, alienation).

Furthermore, it seems to me that there is a very good way to define the difference between individualistic and trans-individualistic behavior. In the first case, other human beings (take, for example, the Oedipus complex) are only *objects* of desire, hate, repulsion or indifference. With regard to the second, we might take an elementary example. If there are two of us involved in lifting a weight, my partner does not have the status of an object in relation to me but is part of the subject of the action, since neither he nor I have lifted this weight by ourselves. *Both* of us have.

It is to such a collective subject that all human behavior with a historical dimension is connected. Included here is technology, social organization and, as we have shown in a number of works, also literary and artistic creation. It is within this dimension that the three linguistic domains of ideology by Umberto Eco are situated: the existence of mental structures or contexts that determine, structure and often deform reception; the chance for certain groups to act, even consciously, through language in order to prescribe specific structures; and finally, the ideological component of language. I would simply add that if these three domains of linguistic action most likely exist in every human society, they are not autonomous. Furthermore, they too are reciprocally influenced. It is, however, essential to study the variable nature of this interaction in each particular case.

I now come to the problem posed in the last talk, which concerns the distinction between artificial and natural language. We all know the extraordinary importance of the role of artificial languages in mathematics, logic and the physico-chemical sciences, as well as their major role in advancing research. Still, who would dare say as much for the human sciences? Certainly, there have been a few attempts but, apart from political economy (and it is probably necessary to limit this exception to the study of market economy), no artificial language seems to be truly functional for these latter disciplines.

This problem goes back to an even more general one: the fact that positivist sociologists, who think they can study human facts with the same methods and techniques as the natural sciences, always fail to understand processes of transformation and a reality that presents itself as more than usually complex. We have recently been given a particularly eloquent example of this. [Here Goldmann cites the failure of sociologists to foresee the events of May 1968 in France.]

This inability to grasp social reality seems to me to lie precisely in the application of methods based on the physico-chemical and natural sciences to a domain that requires completely different methods. At least for the moment, this is also true of attempts to introduce mathematical rigor and artificial languages into this domain. Ultimately, it is a question of the status and nature of objectivity in the two domains, what Hegel called "the subject-object identity," which characterizes the status of the social and historical sciences. It is here, moreover, that one finds the basic opposition between dialectical thought and the Western philosophical tradition of individualism running from Descartes through Kant to Husserl. If, in effect, the subject of thought and action is always transindividual, as Hegel, Marx and other dialectical thinkers would have it, then any consideration of human facts by a subject also involves self-reflection, since the collectivity is both the subject and the object of reflection. According to Marx himself, *Das Kapital* is the working class's analysis of capitalist society, which means the working class's analysis of itself. Here, however, I have proposed a correction. From Hegel to the young Lukacs, most dialectical thinkers have spoken about the subject-object identity without distinguishing one from the other. I have suggested that one speak of a *partial* identity between the two since with each investigation there is a different structure that must be brought to light.

Of course, we must not forget that rigor and precision must remain at the center of all scientific reflection. Nor must we forget that in the historical and social sciences the status and nature of this rigor are different from that in the physico-chemical sciences. All of you are most likely acquainted with Comte's criticism of introspective psychology. One cannot observe one's own anger because his observations are deformed in the process, just as one's anger is modified by the process of observing it. In psychology, researchers have gotten round this problem. They have given up the direct study of consciousness in order to study the behavior of animals and human beings other than themselves. Unfortunately, sociologists cannot make use of such a solution, since to some degree they are always involved in a collectivity which includes the social group to which both they and the group they are studying belong. This is also true of the sociologist concerned with analyzing the most primitive and remote society in as much as he belongs to the human species. Thus, if it is inevitable that the subject and object are partially identical, then at least partially science too is composed of consciousness. To some degree, both researchers and their investigations belong to the reality being studied, so that in the human sciences it is impossible to separate radically judgments of value from judgments of fact. In other words, the sociologist must always avoid two dangers, two illusions: the objectivist illusion and the subjectivist or relativist illusion. The first is based on the methods and aims of the physico-chemical and natural sciences, while the second approximates introspective and intuitive sociological reflection. The dialectical method is the only positive method insofar as it synthesizes science and consciousness and value judgments and judgments of fact.

To take only two examples: at the conclusion of his paper, Mr. Eco criticized positivism and mentioned the danger of exploding the system of signs. He also warned against those who, when talking about social reality, forget that it is always meaningful and always implies language and communication. They are victims of the objectivist illusion, a position wide open to criticism. Conversely, however, one must not reduce reality to communication and language nor think that it can be studied comprehensively on the basis of such a bias. Signs are also signifiers. An explosion of signs is never simply that but refers back to a much deeper and more general explosion which touches upon social reality itself.

Likewise, when existentialist subjectivism and voluntarism were very popular, dialectical thinkers had to defend the *structural* aspect of human behavior against Sartre and his disciples. This involves not only external reality (in Sartrean language: the situation), but also one's thought, behavior and emotions. And now, with the popularity of linguistically inspired structuralism in the human sciences and especially with the highly dogmatic form of the Levi-Straussian and Barthean school, we have found ourselves obliged, in the very name of scientific rigor, to insist on the reality of the *subject* and on the fact that structures are not autonomous realities but are a basic aspect of human thought and behavior. Mr. Benveniste is quite correct in saying that one must study the passage from one structure to another. But this passage is always the result of human action and not that of structures. In the human sciences, scientific thought is always situated between subjectivism and objectivism or, more exactly, at the level of their synthesis.

IV

I am very grateful to Professor Rossi-Landi, who has raised a particularly important theoretical problem that I would like to take up. It seems to me that one must distinguish three different levels in all mental processes: the conscious, the unconscious and the non-conscious. Furthermore, I think that Levi-Strauss's use of the term "unconscious" to designate both the Freudian libido and mental structures (which I have characterized as non-conscious and which have an essentially different status) has created a great deal of confusion.

It is best to limit the term "unconscious" to the Freudian meaning, since it is more or less accepted as part of general usage: that which designates all the tendencies of the libido that have been repressed by social censorship.

Alongside unconscious and conscious psychic processes,... there is an aggregation of mental and even psychic structures, which, without being conscious, are essentially different from the Freudian unconscious. The difference, moreover, is apparent as soon as one considers it. According to the psychoanalytic concept of the libido, one must overcome an obstacle in order to make a repressed desire conscious: the censor. Thanks to Freud and other psychoanalysts, we know the difficulties involved in this process. With regard to non-conscious psychic structures, however, there are no such obstacles in bringing the non-conscious to consciousness. To some extent these structures are similar to muscular and nervous ones in that we are not aware of them. We can easily become so, however, if we wish to study them and make them known, but there is no need here to overcome any censor or prohibition. Still, knowledge of these structures is crucial in comprehending both men's mental processes and their behavior. Professor Rossi-Landi has asked if the various levels of one's mental processes are individual or social.

Here my reply is precise: non-conscious mental structures are totally or almost totally *social*. In practically all of my concrete investigations, I have succeeded in showing that it is through the work's relation to a collective subject, and not to its author, that one can understand the work in a scientifically qualifiable way. I must add, though, that this is only true of major works that are rigorously coherent and which, in our field of study, are equal to the chemist's or physicist's laboratory experiment. As for mediocre works, it is clearly much more difficult to understand them apart from the writer's personality, since to some extent (and at times totally), they are linked to the latter's libidinal forces. Most often, though, this difficulty is due to the fact that such works are a mixture of social mental structures, and every mixture is relatively unique. Therefore, it is not easily given to scientific investigation.

The supposition that an individual can invent a coherent mental structure seems just as improbable as the hypothesis that a single individual can invent such a complex language as French or English. In fact, it is only after thousands of experiments and trials and errors that those mental structures are elaborated that govern our behavior, emotions, thought and creative activity.

Someone has also mentioned the differences that exist between science and art, between the theoretical and the aesthetic. I will reply simply by taking up the position of Kant and Hegel. In both domains man introduces order and unity where there is multiplicity and richness. On the theoretical level, however, he does so through concepts. On the artistic, through the non-conceptual imagination. In Pascal's philosophical thought, for example, there is a discussion of "death." In Racine's *Phèdre* (a literary work that corresponds to Pascalian philosophy), there is not "death" but "the dying Phèdre," a character out of place in the conceptual work of Pascal. Thus, the writer or creative artist, whose consciousness is on the non-conceptual and imaginary level, need not comprehend the objective meaning of his work. In fact, it is essentially the critic's function to bring the latter's meaning to light. It is sufficient for the writer to feel the richness, unity and coherence of his work at the level of aesthetic perception.

I would like to make a final comment on the libidinal and unconscious tendencies studied by psychoanalysts. This unconscoius is no longer purely individual for a twofold reason. First, it is the result of a social repression without which it would be incomprehensible. Second, in achieving a symbolic level of sublimation, it is to a very large extent based on language, which is an eminently social creation.

With regard to the coherent structuring processes of human consciousness, it is of course a mixture of the collective and the individual and libidinal. This mixture differs only according to the person involved. To illustrate this, let us take the two extremes of a line. On the one end, libidinal meaning and behavior dominates so absolutely that the individual's social coherence is disorganized. Here we have the alienated person or the madman. On the other end, the individual's behavior belongs to a rigorous social coherence without in the least modifying or troubling it. Here we have the major philosophical or artistic creations, based respectively on conceptual and imaginary processes. Between these two extremes, we have various mixtures that we represent — you, me, and all the others who are neither alienated nor creative geniuses.

Name Index

Adorno, T.W., 6, 21, 26, 99
Aeschylus, 101, 104
Althusser, L., 37, 43, 47, 50, 87, 149
Arnauld, A., 52, 67
Aron, R., 39

Barcos, p. 52
Barthes, R., 37, 51
Bastide, R., 106, 108
Bell, D., 39
Benveniste, 148, 154
Bergson, H., 46
Boella, I., 6, 9, 12
Bonazis, C., 31

Camus, A., 138
Comte, A., 45, 86, 153
Corti, M., 24
Crouzet, M., 5

Daix, P., 46
De Foe, 6
Descartes, R., 41, 95, 112, 124, 150, 152
Diderot, D., 52
Dilthey, W., 12, 17, 22, 23
Duvignaud, J., 23
Durkheim, E., 45

Eco, U., 151, 153
Escarpit, R., 31

Feuerbach, L., 87, 88
Foucault, M., 36, 37, 43, 51
Freud, S., 47, 48, 59, 92, 93, 94, 97, 98, 105, 106, 109, 120, 124, 125, 155

Galileo, 114
Genet, J., 24, 117, 120-122, 124-127, 130-131, 133-134, 137, 146
Gombrowicz, W., 117, 122-125, 129, 130, 133, 134
Gorz, A., 140

Grahl, B., 6
Gramsci, A., 13, 22, 23
Greimas, A., 37, 149
Groethysen, B., 25
Gurvitch, G., 26

Hegel, G.W.F., 21, 35, 47, 57, 62, 86, 88, 89, 92, 117-118, 147, 150, 152, 156
Heidegger, M., 37
Husserl, E., 9, 26, 44, 150, 152
Hyppolite, J., 112

Jakobson, R., 149
Jaspers, K., 17, 37, 84

Kant, I., 21, 44, 52, 88, 112, 117, 119, 147, 150, 152, 156
Kristeva, J., 120

Lacan, J., 47
Lask, E., 6
Leenhardt, J., 5, 6, 19
Lenin, V.I., 67, 117
Lotman, J., 7, 8, 9, 24, 29, 30, 33
Lotringer, 35, 36
Lukacs, G., 6, 8, 10, 11, 12, 13, 21, 22, 25, 27, 32, 37, 57, 65, 66, 72, 92, 118, 147, 152

Malbranche, 112
Mallet, S., 140
Malraux, A., 120
Marcuse, H., 39, 140
Markus, G., 10
Marx, K., 6, 7, 13, 14, 16, 35, 41, 45, 47, 50, 55, 58, 59, 61, 62, 65, 71, 72, 88, 89, 92, 93, 99, 117, 118, 139, 147, 150, 152
Memmi, A., 26
Molière, J., 121
Morawski, S., 31
Mukarovsky, J., 7, 23

Nicole, 52, 67

Orcibal, M., 80

Palmier, J.-M., 5
Parsons, T., 42
Pascal, B., 21, 44, 45, 48, 52, 63, 67,
  69, 78, 79, 80, 81, 82, 103, 104,
  107, 111, 112, 117, 118, 120, 156
Pavlov, 86
Perse, St. John, 141, 142, 143, 144
Piaget, J., 6, 7, 8, 9, 10, 12, 14, 15,
  16, 19, 21, 22, 25, 32, 55, 56, 58,
  59, 61, 62, 70, 72, 75, 92, 96
Poincaré, H., 44
Pouler, G., 46

Racine, J.B., 42, 43, 44, 45, 46, 48,
  67, 69, 78, 79, 80, 82, 86, 101, 102,
  103, 107, 112, 120, 146, 148, 156
Rickert, H., 6

Ricoeur, P., 91, 99
Riesman, D., 39
Rossi-Landi, F., 30, 154, 155
Ruwet, N., 146, 147

Sartre, J.-P., 36, 37, 41, 53, 73, 74,
  89, 92, 124, 138, 154
Sebeok, T., 150
Simmel, G., 6
Stalin, J., 129

Tell, E., 5
Todorov, T., 149
Trotsky, L., 129

Uspenskij, B., 7, 24, 29, 30

Weber, M., 6, 12, 13
Williams, R., 5